IN WHOSE EYES?

Portrait of a Schizophrenic

by

Anne Bergeron

This book is a work of fiction. Places, events, and situations in this story are purely fictional. Any resemblance to actual persons, living or dead, is coincidental.

ISBN: 0-7596-7751-4

This book is printed on acid free paper.

1stBooks - rev. 01/04/02

TABLE OF CONTENTS

INTRODUCTION v

Chapter 1 - Ok Physically.. 1

Chapter 2 - Not Ok Emotionally.. 8

Chapter 3 - Getting Me Committed 19

Chapter 4 - A County Crisis 26

Chapter 5 - Buckling Down.. 33

Chapter 6 - Finally Rescued 39

Chapter 7 - On The Brink... 46

Chapter 8 - Finding My Niche.. 56

Chapter 9 - The Six Year Build-Up.. 64

Chapter 10 - Moving On... 70

Chapter 11 - Entering The Fray... 82

Chapter 12 - Valentine's Day.. 94

Chapter 13 - Professors And Class Size 108

Chapter 14 - A Bad Impression 119

Chapter 15 - "Go Away And Do Your Thesis!" 129

Chapter 16 - The Downward Spiral....................................... 138

Chapter 17 - Ph.D Economists 149

Chapter 18 - Making A Life 162

Chapter 19 - After Effects 177

Chapter 20 - How To See It... 188

INTRODUCTION

By Kerwin Lebeis, M.D.

WHAT IS SCHIZOPHRENIA?

The term "schizophrenia" suffers as many terms in psychiatry do from meaning many things to many people. The most oft heard derivatives of this term in popular are "schizy" and "schizo" which vary in meaning from referring to a behavior that distances others to one that is the subject of derision due to its oddity. One of the most popular meanings of schizophrenia is a split personality, commonly referred to as multiple personality, but which has no connection with schizophrenia. It is as if we are so embarrassed by mental illness that we do not even want to take the time to learn the proper terminology for it.

Schizophrenia is a pervasive alteration in the entire personality. It usually starts early, cutting off the development of individuals in their teens or 20's and precluding a full, active and rich adult life. The illness does this by altering perception, socialization, thinking, and emotional expression in a way that makes the individual incomprehensible and generally stange and socially unacceptable.

HOW DOES SCHIZOPHRENIA COME ON?

The onset of schizophrenia may be sudden or gradual and its coming is often heralded by prodromal symptoms that do not meet diagnostic criteria for the illness but give a preview of the inability to trust, reason properly, or relate socially that will persist in one form or another throughout the ilness. The difficulties of the schizophrenic start in the sense of reality in which the rest of us are at home. We take for granted the constancy of some perceptions. When we walk into a room in which we have been many times before, we have a comfortable feeling of familiarity. The same holds true when we see a loved one, sense our bodies, observe the relation of the earth below to the sky above, hear a familiar melody or background sound, smell or taste a usual fare. Eventually in the topsy turvy world of the schizophrenic any constancy, whether it is provided by delusions, strange postures and behaviors, or hallucinations, which may be proprioceptive, visceral, visual, auditory, olfactory, tactile or gustatory, is preferable to such a loss of reference points and boundaries.

Early on in life we do not have a clear idea of where we leave off and others begin. If the breast shows up every time we are hungry, we as infants might assume it is part of us. The schizophrenic has lost this when perceptions do not fit together and must leave open the question of whether the perceptions arise from the actions of others or of the individual.

WHERE DID THE CONCEPT OF SCHIZOPHRENIA COME FROM?

The concept of schizophrenia started as a reasonably specific illness described in the 1800's as a deterioration of personallity with preservation of intellect. It was expanded for a time to include all sorts of serious psychiatric ilness during the first half of the 1900's, especially in America under the influence of psychoanalysis, which emphasezed the continuum between less severe mental illness known as neurosis and more severe ones known as psychosis. This all changed with the advent of specific treatment for another severe mental illness, manic depressive illness, or bipolar disorder as it is now known. That treatment is lithium, which made it important to distinguish bipolar disorder from schizophrenia. Using a more narrow definition of schizophrenia a World Health Organization study has shown that schizophrenia exists in all cultures at an incidence of between one half and one percent of the population.

The narrow definition of schizophrenia excludes prominent depression or mania. An intermediary condition called schizoaffective disorder has the persistent thinking disorder of schizophrenia in between major episodes of mania or depression. Schizoaffective disorder is a heterogenous illness since the prognosis of the depressed variety is closer to schizophrenia while the form which has manic episodes has a prognosis closer to bipolar disorder in which 60 to 80 percent of patients will substantially improve with treatment.

WHERE HAS SCHIZOPHRENIA GONE?

In contrast to the many times spectacular response to treatment of its sister psychosis bipolar disorder, schizophrenia has responded less well to treatment. This lesser response has fueled research looking for structural brain damage as reflected in the size of the brain and its natural cavities called ventricles since structural damage, as opposed to a mere chemical imbalance, could not possibly be reversed with medication. This research has led to only equivocally positive results showing structural changes in the brains of schizophrenics.

The treatment of schizophrenia until recently has been more effective in correcting what are termed positive as opposed to negative symptoms. Negative symptoms are those that reflect a deficit in function such as inability to form relationships, express emotions, or generate spontaneous logical thinking. Positive symptoms are the florid ones that are easy to identify as mental illness such as hallucinations, delusions which are fixed, false beliefs, or agitation. Schizophrenia has not gone away with treatment, it is just a quieter illness.

WHAT CAUSES SCHIZOPHRENIA?

Schizophrenia is thought to be the result of a combination of genetic and perinatal influences. It is likely a group of related illnesses. Perinatal influences are anything that can insult or retard the development of the early brain including infectious, toxic, physical, metabolic, and nutrition-related factors. Traces of these influences may persist into adulthood in the form of the so-called "soft neurological signs," which are signs of mild dysfunction of the nervous system such as uneven or unsymmetrical motor, sensory, or coordination performance.

The evidence for the genetic transmission of schizophrenia, while as strong as that for most medical illnesses, led to the concept of schizophrenic spectrum disorders. Schizophrenia occurs at a very low rate in families but odd behavior and unusual socialization is fairly common in families of schizophrenics. This odd personality disorder, now termed schizotypal, when lumped together with schizophrenia showed a stronger genetic component to the genesis of schizophrenia.

WHERE ARE THE SCHIZOPHRENICS?

As a result of concerns about the legal rights of mental patients in the 1970's, many seriously ill patients were released from mental institutions to presumably be treated in community mental health centers. The status of the schizophrenic is not functionally different due to this change and what has been gained is the "right" to wander the streets given the schizophrenic's propensity to avoid social interaction. Instead of being hidden away from society in mental institutions, schizophrenics who are ill are now hidden in the ranks of the new group that is the focus of social concern in America in the 1900's, namely the homeless. It is almost as if the pendulum has swung in America from calling everything schizophrenia in the first half of the century to denying its existence as a potentially debilitating and chronic illness in the last quarter of the century.

WHAT CAN BE EXPECTED FROM TREATMENT?

Haven't we all known someone who needed treatment but was opposed to it? Unfortunately, no mental treatment works instantaneously so the patient needs to "sit still." This is particularly challenging for someone whose desire to be part of a society, which may be the main impetus for initiating treatment, is marginal. The mainstay of pharmacological treatment are medications called anti-psychotics which are patterned in their actions on chlorpromazine or Thorazine which has been used since the 1950's. Anti-psychotics are more than just tranquillizers. They have specific effects on hallucinations and delusions. The newer anti-psychotics have fewer side effects such as dry mouth, blurred vision, constipation, and hypotension than Thorazine but do not have significantly different actions. Any success of one anti-psychotic medication over another is related to unknown or "idiosyncratic" factors. In addition, long term use of anti-psychotics can damage nerves which can lead to persistent twitches, writhing movements and intermittent protrusion of the tongue. The exception is clozapine or Clozaril which has few side effects such as excess salivation and a blood disorder called agranulocytosis, but which has benefitted many with resistant negative symptoms. The conventional wisdom says that a third get better, a third stay the same, and a third get worse and we are always fighting to beat those odds.

WHAT ELSE CAN BE DONE?

In a disease which can be as devastating as schizophrenia there is always the question of what more can be done. The hope of the family and the patient needs to be nurtured without giving unwarranted encouragement for the pursuit of every unproven treatment. The modern treatment of mental illness recognized the importance of approaching the problem from all angles, vocational, avocational, social, interactional, familial, and so on. Because the schizophrenic can be overwhelmed by too much stimuli, all these approaches must be tempered and paced to what the patient can tolerate. Too much criticism and complaint in the environment is noxious to the schizophrenic. A measured approach to treatment is not just "good" it is crucial to making as much progress as possible.

WHAT IS IN THE FUTURE?

The most exciting part of the story about schizophrenia is the advances in the understanding of the molecular biology. Thorazine is known to block nerve cell or neuron transmissions based on dopamine. When dopamine is too low in a part of the brain called the basal ganglia, parkinsonism results. One of the side effects of Thorazine is a pseudo-parkinsonism. The dopamine theory of schizophrenia states that there are excesses of dopamine in certain areas of the brain such as the septal area which lead to schizophrenia. As of yet we do not have a drug-induced model of schizophrenia. Drugs which increase biogenic amines such as amphetamine do cause paranoia and drugs that alter perceptions such as phencyclidine can mimic some of the behavior in schizophrenia, but no drug has been able to duplicate the whole picture. There are other difficulties with the dopamine theory since the behavior of the receiving neuron may be more important than how much dopamine is sent to it. When the receiving neuron is chronically exposed to too much dopamine, the number of its receptors decrease and the nerve itself may shrink as the number of nerve endings decrease. Clozaril may take advantage of the downstream neuron's ability to be influenced.

While the exact definitions of mental illnesses will shift over time, the research focus is on drugs which will alter brain chemicals whose functions reach across diagnostic categories. The lines between formal mental illnesses and minor mental problems will be blurred over time, the question remains why these traits exist in any of us.

WHY DOES SCHIZOPHRENIA EXIST?

Ethologists study how species as whole are governed and, absent definitive proof, speculate on reasons for various behaviors and traits. What is good for the preservation of a species and a specific individual can be entirely different. Metaphorically speaking, species have a very simple answer to the age old question about how the good of the many can be reconciled with the good of the few or the one. The species are always engineering for the former. That means that if a few schizophrenics or all of them need to be sacrificed they will be if only to get the benefit of an occasional schizophrenic or genetically related "spectrum disorder" whose unusual approach to a problem may benefit the entire species. It is ironic that the odd perceptions that reek so much havoc in individual lives might provide the basis for solving a problem that the species needs solved. In a sense we all may "owe" the schizophrenic.

WHAT IS TO BE GAINED FROM SCHIZOPHRENIA?

There are several things to be learned from the study of schizophrenia. Since it is one of the most feared mental illnesses, study can replace unrealistic fears with knowledge of its possible beneficial effects on our society. The moral and ethical argument is that we need those less fortunate than us to test and provide a forum for good works for us. Besides that, we could all benefit from a little of that odd perceptual framework to question the unproductive stereotypes and modern insistence that the individual do it all on his or her own. Mental illnesses such as depression carry the stigma that prevents treatment, relief of suffering, and achievement of full potential. One key to the future is molecular biology, which examines how simple molecules can have widespread effects on behavior. For every schizophrenic a dozen and more of the rest of us have lesser emotional ills, most of which go untreated or undertreated due in large part to ignorance, fear, and prejudice. If our society is to reach its full potential, it will have to stop cutting off its nose to keep its face.

CHAPTER 1

OK PHYSICALLY

I worry too much, that's one problem. And I analyze things to death, always trying to figure out what I'm supposed to do. Then of course I play right into the hands of anyone plotting for or against me. Later, unfailingly, I hope I did the right thing. I guess I'm what you call a "good person."

Another way of putting it is that I'm easily manipulated. And paranoid. Very un-"Zen" of me not being more mindful in my day-to-day life. But then again that must be what happens with schizophrenia.

Why I got so obsessed at college I don't know. Certainly deciding to finish the degree was a positive thing. I had goofed off back when I was a freshman in school year 1970-71. Now at 26 years old in fall 1978 I thought sure I could handle the challenge. Look at what I had had to put up with in my various jobs, I thought. Nothing to scoff at.

Since life in a big city had left me feeling somewhat jaded, I had to summon up all of my enthusiasm for this big push. So I went overboard in the opposite direction. I wanted to be noticed as a hot shot student. (So insecure.)

And it was easy for me to be transformed into a "fact processor", taking profuse notes and writing long answers on tests. "It was all there, Anne," said one Ph.D student teacher after a test, and I was so proud of that. What a setting to go crazy in, though—the "inner sanctum" of offices and classrooms on the campus of a well-thought-of university. At least it seemed that way to me.

The strange truth about my "case" only became obvious to me years after the fact, but the summer sessions of 1980 were ground zero, I know that. I latched onto a professor of economics named Malcom Collins. Truth be told, in some ways I was in love with him. Kind of a school girl crush, though it really ended up spawning something a lot more dangerous.

When he asked me if I knew what I was "getting into" with him as my thesis advisor, I said yes, though I actually thought he meant all the rigorousness. Just his asking that question should have been a sign to me that something was amiss. Throughout this unfortunate relationship, I alternated between being a savvy player and an innocent ditz. I thought the whole honors degree thing would be "fun." That's really about how far ahead I looked. A silly and distant thought was that maybe some day I'd get a Ph.D.

I liked to take on challenges, but was not always up for the hard work and mental acuity required. I looked up to people I thought were "brilliant in their field," and had actually been obsessed with a professor at a big university before. I was easily impressed.

At Tydings it was Malcom who caught my eye. Later I thought that various people at that university had set me up to run through a maze where "significant" others could look down and see me trying to scratch my way out. The eerie thing was that maybe that was true.

But Malcom's reaction to me and my personality was rather underhanded—he certainly didn't play fair. And like I said, I'm easy to influence. I got caught hook, line, and sinker thinking I was so smart when actually I wasn't. Obviously that was upsetting to me. To say the least, in the end the pressure of an unbelievable college effort and an inappropriate preoccupation with "powerful" people led me down a road that would eventually cause me to go over board. This story lies there.

***

Looking a full year after my regrettable college days, while I was desperately trying to find my way out of the mess I got myself into during 1980, I didn't spend much time thinking real thoughts. So, as ridiculous as it sounds, in June 1981 I went on a fast so I could get "rescued" from my "romantic" situation with the said Malcom Collins. Somehow I believed that could happen. While June 1980 was ground zero, June 1981 nearly was the end of my life. Now that would have been tragic.

In any case, while I looked normal at 130 pounds in May 1981, in 38 days I had starved myself down to around 95. I had thought hard to know what was the truth, what comes next, not realizing that nobody cared half as much about me and my fantasy life as I thought they did. Where's my July rent check? is what the landlords must have thought. What the hell was that? was probably what my husband Todd was thinking.

But it was the 38th day of the non-eating fiasco when Todd and then the cops showed up at my locked and chained door. The first person to try to talk to me was Todd; he was almost crying. I heard him and panicked.

When I tried to stand, my knees buckled under my weight. Maybe I had stood up too fast. I fell back on the couch, feeling really weak for the first time in that exile mode of living. It was like I hadn't realized what I had been doing to my body all that time. Todd was begging me to open the door and I was tempted, but I thought, no, he's the wrong person. I was so stubborn and really hunkered down into what I was thinking.

But I did finally wobble to my feet and grabbed a bottle filled with water and took a drink. I yelled at him, "Just go away," but a few seconds later the water quickly came right back up. With my paranoia in full bloom, I actually yelled at Todd, saying "See, you made me sick!"

I realized that I was being cruel, but I had already come to terms in those 38 days to giving up Todd. Deluded by my various fantasies, it had made me cry that I would not be "allowed" to see him again. I thought that didn't seem right, because in large part we were good friends to each other anyway. But me being beyond "off the wall" at this point, I thought

Malcom was in love with me, no more Todd, and I actually broke down.

Not that day, though. I was too busy starving for God's sake! And what the hell was taking everyone so long? I imagined people right outside, waiting in the wings to see how I "performed."

Actually, Malcom sounds like a real jerk. All the things I "believed" about him. Not letting me see Todd again? Not wanting me to get a degree? What did I like about him? should have been the real question. It seems obvious that I never asked myself that very thing.

Once Todd left, I settled back on my couch. I still had the water bottle and was watching my abdomen bloat up as I drank. It was fascinating. Suddenly, I heard a key turn in my door, though thank God there was a chain. "Police-let us in!" they yelled. I told them to wait while I dressed.

Now they're getting really melodramatic, I thought. Police trying to break in? But there were a few pieces of clothing left after "the purge," so I just put on a nightgown and sweater and answered the door. I left the chain on at first.

There stood the two policemen. "There are a lot of people out here who are concerned about your well-being," they said. I smiled and thought, of course there are. I was a famous person, wasn't I?

I also laughed at what I thought was a subtle gesture the "people" had gone through of sending one policeman with a Lawrence, Massachusetts accent. A nice touch. I would always know that sound, since that was the city where I was born and where a lot of my relatives lived.

One policeman said, "Your husband wanted us to see if you were all right, if you were sick or in any other trouble." I said something dumb about they must be doctors, but they smiled at me anyway. As far as they knew I might have <u>always</u> weighed 95 pounds. "We were just checking," the Lawrence cop said. They handed me some telegrams and turned to leave after apologizing for intruding. As they left, I heard one of them say to the other, "She seems OK physically, but not emotionally." Quite a thumbnail sketch. But I was glad to lock the door.

Since I had not let Todd see me, I just knew the three of them would be back interfering with my destiny that tied me to "my" professor. It was definitely time to get out of my "efficient" apartment, knowing I would never return.

My landlords had just come by a few days before the encounter with Todd and the policemen to "talk" to me since I hadn't paid my July rent. They said they would help me out in any way they could. After the meeting with the police, I decided to let them do just that. I plugged in my telephone and contacted them.

The landlords seemed glad to hear from me. No doubt they were nervous about a renter who acted so strangely. Yes, of course they would let me have my $200 back. (They later got it from Todd.) Sure, they could go to the grocery store. I asked for a duffle bag to carry my things, a bar of Caress soap and some things to eat: a nectarine, a Hostess cherry pie and chocolate milk. I was hungry and got excited about the prospect of eating again.

I also told them to simply ring the doorbell the next morning to let me know that they had come by with my food and so on. After that, they could come back in an hour. That would give me time to eat and shower for the first time in over a month. I went back to lay on the couch one last time before being "ready." I kept my nightgown and sweater on just in case there were any more people wondering to themselves about me.

I woke up at dawn the next morning at my arranged time. Why so early, I don't know. Although I had mixed feelings about leaving, I was thinking more about instant gratification-in otherwords food. I let my taste buds run wild, especially savoring the thought of chocolate milk. When the landlords showed up, they had everything I had asked for. Speaking through the closed door, I told them thanks for going to the grocery store.

The first thing I did after gathering up my things was eat. The nectarine wasn't fully ripe and seemed to have a lemony taste. But the cherry pie and chocolate milk had it too, though I ate and drank all of it. It probably had something to do with the fast. In any case, later I took a shower and stuffed whatever was left over into the duffle bag that for some reason read "The New York Times." Then I waited for a knock on the door from my landlords. At one point one of the landlords had said something about "Maybe we should all wear masks."

During the interlude, though, I kept thinking that getting together with Malcom was certainly becoming complex. I would soon meet up with him though; I was sure of it.

The landlords came and slipped my money under the door. I told them to wait around the corner until I left. When they thought I was gone (I was on the stairwell), they opened the apartment door and one of them said, "Boy, she really cleaned this place out!" I had—all of it down the garbage chute.

But I was on my way out. I opened the door that led out to the alley below the apartments. I had looked out on that alley many times during my stay there. I had on a saved dress I had made and carried the heavy bag over my shoulder. It seemed strange that I had brought along my make-up mirror. Why hadn't that been thrown away?

The weather was muggy outside, a July day in Washington, D.C. Flowers dotted the walls once I made the left turn out of the alley. I walked to a bus that was a few stops down from where I would usually have been picked up. I didn't want anyone to recognize me, not that they would anyhow. But in my mind I was to be off on a plane to Phoenix from where my sisters and mother had been sending telegrams.

The whole thing with Malcom was really confusing, almost implausible, though that can happen. I hadn't had anyone with whom to bounce off my theories about what was going on, and my thoughts had consumed me for 38 days and more. Still, I had put myself back on line and was "up and about" in a way that surprised a few psychiatrists who learned about it later. Finally, a bus came along and I climbed aboard. Another journey was beginning.

CHAPTER 2

NOT OK EMOTIONALLY

My life starting in summer and fall 1980 could have been described as a "constant psychotic break that was running its course unchecked." That was when my mental stability completely broke down. Prior to that, and even with some eccentric behavior, I seemed to hold on. But only tenuously. By September of 1980, though, a few students and teachers who knew me were asking me what had happened over the summer. Why the strained look on my face? Why so withdrawn? Had something bad happened?

But by the time I moved out of my house with Todd and into my Washington, D.C. apartment in May 1981, I was already seriously delusional. By then, my schizophrenia had existed for at least eleven months. And even though I was fired from my research assistant job the day before my move, I rationalized moving as a quick fix to link me with the "right" person.

I further rationalized that having no income for the time being was all right. So big deal that I was moving into a new apartment with no money. To top things off, I even referred to my husband (when speaking to the two young landlords) as "just being a friend." At one point, I think they took that the wrong way. But from that day of Todd helping me move in, we would be separated for six months.

My day-to-day life in May 1981 was uncomplicated. Although unemployed and without a car, I had saved all of my money from the research job, so that wasn't a problem. There was a food store half a block away, where I bought different kinds of sauces, along with fruit, and beer was easily carried home.

Next to that was an Italian restaurant where Todd took me out for my birthday. It was delicious too, us sharing some stranger things like anti-pasto or a more ordinary plate of spaghetti and meatballs. There was also a movie theater, where I only saw one bad movie, an Irish bar (how tempting to a drunk like me), and a little further down, the very entertaining National Zoo.

The walk up and down that stretch of Connecticut Avenue became very familiar to me. About twice a week I went to the zoo to see the two pandas and the golden colored bears that I liked so much. Things seemed "normal" and sometimes, after looking around, I would sit on the lawn so everyone could see me at peace with myself. I thought I was "charmed." Actually, I just had delusions of grandeur.

A few weeks after I moved, my birthday came around. Though Todd and I were keeping a congenial distance, we got together for dinner. It was nice not to be alone on that day. After dinner I invited Todd to my apartment. He was a little uncomfortable there, not knowing what our roles should be. "I guess you're not interested in making love, are you?" he asked. I really wasn't, although it was nothing personal. I just had somebody else in mind. Even though Malcom and I wouldn't "get together" until school let out for the summer, I was building up to that. I had to be ready to follow all the right "rules."

There again, who was I infatuated with? Why would I even consider getting together with somebody who would make all the moves or have me under his thumb? I had gotten used to an equal partnership with Todd, and he and I got along real well. It would be a long time before I would realize what I had, but by then too, Todd would have changed himself. After the mental illness began, even he had a problem understanding it.

Everything seemed normal to me while I was living at that efficiency apartment. My last semester at college was hell compared to the freedom that I had during May 1981. I filled all of my waking hours with pleasantries, and everything had a subtle purpose. It was at this time that I was already thinking about throwing everything away.

9

Once Todd walked me home after I fainted inside that nearby theater. It happened after a scene where Sean Connery got a long needle pushed right into his jugular vein and I just couldn't stand it. So there we were back in my apartment again. Later I would reflect back on the times I had let Todd into my place and decided that I needed to be "punished" because of that. In my delusional frame of mind, it wasn't right for me to accept kindness from any man other than Malcom. What could I have been thinking?

Another time, I met Todd at the National Gallery of Art. While strolling through the gallery, he asked me whether it was over with us. I thought it was and told him so. He said there were a lot of "foxes" around. His reason for mentioning that I didn't know.

My life could have gone on indefinitely like that, waiting for Malcom and socializing with my husband, but one day a bizarre thing happened. I caught the bus headed downtown to my bank. As I grabbed a handle to hold onto, I looked outside and saw Malcom waiting for a bus right behind mine. I tried to get off my bus to go to him, but didn't make it in time. As I stared out the back window, I saw that he must have caught that next bus and was going to follow me—or so I assumed.

My mind was racing. I decided to get off the bus to see if Malcom would get off too. I looked back at his bus and he had. Or at least I thought so. I walked away from him as he "followed" me. Suddenly, I turned around and headed back towards him. He turned and disappeared around a corner. I was enthralled. He was actually looking for me in downtown D.C.

As it turned out, it probably wasn't him, a much as I wanted to believe it was. It was a hallucination, one of the only ones I could point to later and say ha, there was one.

But it all pointed to my shame, and how I felt about my actions during those last sessions in college. That's how I analyzed the throwing everything away and moving to an apartment and so on. I had betrayed my husband, I had been a

10

drunk, etc. Alcohol was a big part of all of the tumultuous history of my life. And it wouldn't be for six years that I gave the stuff up.

During the May purge, I thought the hardest thing to throw away would be my class notes. I had always done such a good job of getting down the gist of everything. But although they were a treasure to me, I was sure that they more than anything else would proved that I was a "phony" in getting a degree.

It's so easy to look back and cringe at the kind of thoughts I had, but at the time I really did believe that Malcom wanted a stay-at-home kind of wife. I must have also thought he wanted a wife with only a high school diploma. I guess I wasn't fazed by the fact that I had already graduated from college.

But in any case I threw my notes out. I would grab up an armful and run down the hall to the garbage chute. Later I threw away my "raw data," etc. Everything gone.

After the class note purge I knew I was on the edge of something serious. I asked Todd for advice. He drove over quickly and, after sitting down in my apartment and looking around, we went down to the basement where the big garbage bin was. Todd, tall enough to reach over and grab the papers, pulled out some calculus notes. I said to forget it. He kept pulling out more notes and I kept saying to forget it.

One thing was that I hadn't yet thrown out my textbooks and I told Todd he could have them. Then, after he lugged them all out to the car, I decided he would not be "allowed" to save those. Todd, being a kind person, dragged them all back in for me to dispose of after he was gone. It was a terrible waste all the stuff I did in that stupid apartment.

Once Todd left, I was about to go completely over the brim into the disaster that had become my life. I then vowed to keep mine and Malcom's "business" to myself. I decided I wouldn't even get my mail.

Prior to leaving my apartment to return home, Todd had looked into my refrigerator and cabinets, probably to see if I had food. That didn't strike me as strange until later. But, since he knew I was "safe," I could be left alone without worrying anybody. This is what I thought while laying around and not eating for over a month after the purge ended.

It was around May 30, 1981, that I decided to go on a complete fast starting on June 1st. I had some chicken drumsticks left, so I baked them and ate them slowly, thinking I wouldn't miss those so much anyway. After that, I threw away all of my pots and pans, kitchenware and all the food.

This is the kind of thing I would think would have been fun to theorize with with the many psychiatric people I talked to after I landed in the county crisis clinic. Why no food for 38 days? Well, that's an interesting question. Did food play a big role in your life when you were a little girl? and that kind of thing. But except for Dr. Crow, my future psychiatrists never really wanted to "talk".

One unnerving thing is that for schizophrenia, HMO insurance companies won't pay for "psychotherapy" of the most familiar kind, with patients discussing dreams or their childhoods or other, more esoteric subjects. Freud said it was a wasted effort on schizophrenics, and I do believe this is one reason people are so afraid of chronically mentally ill people. It's that unpredictability. We're just all off the mark, and parents didn't play any role except for genetics. I would run up against so much discrimination in the future because I wasn't just neurotic (safe), I was at times psychotic (dangerous). Or so I think this is how people feel.

Back to the story, I then started to throw out any remnants of my university degree. For some reason I didn't have my diploma, but I went ahead recklessly and threw away everything else.

The day after I had eaten the rest of my food, I found that I only had 33 cents left if I wanted to buy any. It was May 31, and the federal government was closed, so I went out and searched for something cheap to eat. I took my change and a gold chain that I had gotten from my in-laws for graduation. Since my necklace was just "gold filled," it was worth nothing. Nobody wanted to give me money for my gold wedding ring either.

Since I couldn't ask Todd (another man) for money, I had to deal with my decision never to go back to my bank. Ever since the "Malcom sighting" I had stayed away from all banks. It's almost funny. Anyway, I walked up and down Connecticut Avenue, ending up buying a banana in that grocery store right near my apartment.

That first day of the fast, June 1, 1981, was very easy. I had plenty of cold water and lots of cigarettes, so I was all set. In fact, as always, I just kept myself busy thinking about Tydings University. What could be brewing over there? Why in the world was Malcom following me downtown?

My continuous psychotic break was working hard on my brain and at the same time my "throw away" mode was continuing. I got paranoid about having anything of mine left that wouldn't be appreciated by my "husband." And at that point I wasn't sure who my "husband" was. There was the supervisor at the research firm that got added to the mix. It was so dumb. I think I even found it within me to tell Todd something like "three strikes you're out." There was Professor Brown, Professor Collins and now Michael, the supervisor from where I was fired from a month before. I had some nerve.

One day I met a psychiatrist who was taking over my session for one week and his quick read was, "You think you're in love with men you work with." That kind of took me aback. Well, I guess you could stretch that one out to that point. Yes, I sometimes got infatuated with "unavailable" men. The "old" me anyway.

During all of this there was Todd, who I really believed had always loved me ever since we met. How was this kind of revelation affecting him and his ego? However, at the time I was too self-centered to worry about Todd. I took him for granted.

I was in the middle of throwing everything away when I came to my high school yearbooks, all signed and in good shape. I thought, well in high school I had crushes on boys I knew, etc., so out with all four of them. Things were getting pretty thin when I also started throwing out the clothes I had bought with "Todd's money." Virtually all of them. I would run down the hallways with bunches of clothes, and threw them down the chute, hangers and all. It was a shame, because there were a lot of classic clothes in there.

Life became increasingly bizarre. I had a husband who would give anything to be back in my life, but I was yearning for a professor who wanted nothing to do with me. But back then I was thinking he was following me in buses downtown. So at that time, I didn't feel off the wall in any way; and every day I believed I was pushing ahead dramatically to get things straightened out.

As I've said, the thing that allowed me to virtually disappear for 38 days was that I paid the June rent on time. Nobody would be thinking about me in that way. Plus, Todd had seen that I had all that food. So by July, when I was wasted away, I didn't pay my rent because I was out of money. I had also thrown away all of my checks. So by that time, my landlords caught up with me. But in June, I was utterly alone.

June 5, 1981 was a day I'll always remember. I was so hungry, it was almost unbearable. I would never feel that way again, even though I kept on fasting for 33 more days. But on June 5th my stomach would not quiet down. Since I had not yet thrown away my camera, I called up a sandwich shop across the street to see if I could trade it for a meatball sub. It must have sounded odd to them, and they asked me if I was a "regular customer." I was dumb enough to say no, and that was the end of that. To curb the hunger pangs that day, I went to sleep, even though it was the middle of the day. I didn't cry, I just shut down.

By June 1981, I had been seriously psychotic since the summer of 1980. Almost a year before. My energy had become entangled with thoughts of that professor. I began to believe that somehow I might actually be Collins' wife rather than Todd's. All of this in spite of the fact that Malcom and I never even shook hands. Despite my psychosis and during fall semester 1980 I took tests, took notes, got two A's, 3 B's and one incomplete in my last semester. Apparently, part of my mind was still functioning as normally as I ever am trying to learn something difficult.

During my starvation days, I listened to noises around me. For hours I let the phone ring incessantly until I finally disconnected it. Presumably, I knew that Malcom wouldn't be using the phone to contact me. And Todd wasn't somebody I felt I should keep in contact with since he was aware of my "relationship" with Malcom. My paranoia told me that I shouldn't have given Todd my number. What had he done wrong? I ask myself in retrospect. But all the angst I had inside me was causing me to self-destruct.

Around the second week of the fast, I knew that I had become "famous," that everybody knew everything about me. More delusions of my big ego built up. I had rushed down the hall of my apartment building, arms full of my life's belongings, to throw away, and each trip down that hall was "meaningful" to me in one way or another. Here I am throwing away everything having to do with my honor's thesis, and so on. All of this was very vital to me at the time.

Ironically, part of my later adjustment to my mental illness was coming to terms with having thrown everything away, just like it must be when people's homes burn down. It was all gone. This was to become very depressing to me after a time, but was especially unfortunate that I had to dwell so much on that when I first went back to be with Todd in D.C. in October 1981.

After about two weeks of perfect nothingness in that apartment, I was so wrapped up in my self-imposed isolation, I began to fantasize about a man who lived downstairs who was keeping track of me. He was "watching me" day to day to see how well I was buckling under the stress of my high position. I knew he was a cynic where I was involved. It's just another example of me being a "bad girl" in my own mind. Why was I so selfish, cutting off the people who loved me? All for the extremely fleeting possibility that this professor cared at all about my well-being?

But the "neighbor" downstairs, (the evil person I created in my mind), was sure, I thought, that I would never do the "honorable" thing and just give up. For some reason I thought he knew me well. And true enough, I never wanted to give up my fantasies. But I became convinced that he could be confused into thinking that I had moved or was otherwise gone. This, I thought, would help me somehow. So I tried to keep very still.

Gradually, I got used to existing in such a controlled environment: quiet and dark. I had shut the blinds around June 1, so just little slits of light crept through. Nights turned into mornings, mornings into afternoons, and all around me I could hear everything meshing together. For further quiet, I didn't even use my air conditioning. So add heat to the punishment I was giving myself back then.

Shortly after throwing everything out, I heard the garbage trucks moving around outside. Those involved with my well-being were taking my things somewhere safe, I thought, for when I would join Malcom. Then the two of us could go through my "treasures" together and decide what to keep. In the end, my view of the purge changed, in part because I knew that nobody who loved me would have encouraged me to throw everything away.

Throughout the whole time I was there, I must have been hearing voices too, though I routinely denied that to psychiatrists later, mostly because what my family had claimed when I was first committed. I didn't hear anyone addressing me during the fast, though I did hear the employees from the consulting firm talking about me inside an apartment nearby. I thought that I could distinguish one voice from another, and that they were keeping tabs on me since I got fired from their firm. I believed they must have felt sorry for me, worried that the long-awaited "reunion" with me and Collins might somehow be jeopardized. It's an understatement to say I had obviously lost all touch with reality by then.

By the end of June, I had become very thin and accustomed to my daily routine: lying there listening to the world go by. I knew I had plenty of time left before I would die, I thought, since those Irish Republican Army men had held out for 60 days before they did. At the same time, I thought that I had been carrying on with the starvation game long enough to have produced some results. But why was it ending with Todd and the two policemen at my door? That just didn't seem natural, as if anything was normal about me in that situation.

I was so body conscious that throughout my fast I kept lifting up my legs to see if all the fat was gone; and there were still fleshy areas remaining. I believed at times that I could actually feel the fat inside my body draining out. Although my faith in the Malcom obsession was ridiculous, I didn't see it that way. He would be very "strict" with me. To this day, I cannot explain my infatuation with him. What I should have learned about him by July 1981 was that he was a jerk who played a devious role in dragging me down to the depths I found myself in. Looking back, it all seems so simple.

Prior to my confrontation with Todd and the policemen, I thought I had actually heard Malcom come up to my door one day and speak my name. Excited, I jumped up quickly and opened the door. When nobody was there, I thought he must have been banned from the place where I was living as a "single woman." I also knew that the fast couldn't continue for much longer. I hadn't even been drinking water for about six or seven days. I thought the man who lived downstairs wasn't happy with me simply not eating, he wanted to see me do without water as well. As if I wanted a date with death.

I later wondered about what must have happened in June during my ordeal. Todd's birthday had come and gone, and so had Father's Day. I hadn't even thought about my dad. I remember thinking that soon after being up off the couch. I later found out that my mother was the one who finally put her foot down about me being essentially missing from the face of the earth. My family told Todd to get the cops and get in there, force me out. They knew something was wrong, or I would have sent a card. Little did they know that I was so far off base that it was a miracle that I was still alive. Many thanks to my Mom and Dad.

CHAPTER 3

GETTING ME COMMITTED

I wonder what would have happened if I had opened the door for Todd? He would have known immediately that I hadn't eaten for some time, given my appearance. But would he have realized I had lost touch with reality? If he did recognize psychosis when he saw it, would he have been forceful enough to get me psychiatric help? No one will ever know.

But I was "OK" and enroute to the airport to escape Washington, D.C. But there was a new problem: I didn't have enough money for a one-way flight to Phoenix. On a whim, I took an expensive taxi ride from the airport to a Trailways bus depot. I was tired of dragging that duffle bag around. Although I was close to Todd's workplace once I arrived, I knew better than to contact him. It was his fault that I was leaving D.C. Or so I thought.

I was in a dress for the bus ride, though no other women were, and I would be in it for four days. I kept catching glimpses of myself in the various bus depot restrooms, and was happy that I had finally lost all of that weight.

The worst food in the world had to be at the bus depots. It was all you could buy too, since they were all in remote places. After fasting for 38 days, you would think I'd relish everything I ate, but I didn't. By the time I reached my parents home, I was even more obsessed with food. But I wanted good food, like my parents make.

During the bus ride, I wanted to sit alone and luckily the buses weren't usually filled. When they were, some very heavy women who traveled together, would seek out the skinny people like me to sit next to. I cried one night when a huge woman decided to sleep, leaning over on me and snoring loudly. Actually, I cried partly for the benefit of the people "watching over me." I wanted a report to be made to the "groups" from Washington, D.C. who were watching me through "correspondents." I saw men go to the phones every time we stopped, and believed they were getting in touch with Malcom to report my progress. I thought I was the center of attention. My paranoia was in high gear.

The long bus ride finally came to an end after four days, pulling into the Phoenix depot on Sunday, July 12, at 6:00 a.m. I hadn't slept for four days and instead of phoning my family to pick me up, I waited to see what would happen. Sure enough, I saw people heading towards the telephones. Hungry, I bought some custard, hoping the food in the Phoenix depot might taste better. It didn't. To show the people in the cafeteria that I didn't want anyone to sit with me, I put my purse on the chair to my right. I was still waiting—for what, I didn't quite know.

Suddenly, I saw a thin man's arm swoop down on my purse. I followed the arm up and out of the cafeteria, running and screaming: "Stop that man! He stole my purse!" As I ran out the front doors, I saw the man crouched on his knees by somebody who had stopped him. I pulled my purse out of the thief's hands and shouted "Creep!" before going back in. I didn't even look at his face.

People started gravitating around me, asking about the man. I felt nervous and queasy and decided it was time to catch a cab to my parents' house. On the way out, a police officer asked where I could be reached if the arrest ever led to a court hearing. Not knowing it would come back to haunt me, I gave him my parents' number. Then I took another expensive taxi ride to my parents' home. I knocked on the front and the back door. There was no answer. Finally, I knocked on the window of my parents' bedroom, and my mother peered out. I waved. She cried: "Look Joseph—It's Anne!"

My family was startled at how thin I was. I told them about my 38 day fast, and then started talking about food, food my parents used to make. How I would love some "buckwheat pancakes." How I would love a big spaghetti dinner, etc. I told them that I hadn't slept or showered in four days, and they told me to go and take a shower and relax. My sister Jane gave me some shorts and a top, since all I had left were those few things in the duffle bag. I thought Jane had always been so thin. But after I took a shower and dressed, the clothes fit. It was only then that I realized how much weight I had actually lost.

After dressing, I went into the family room where my mother had just hung up the phone. "You called Todd, didn't you?" I asked, accusingly.

"Yes, he's been very worried about you. Doesn't he deserve at least that?" my mother replied.

I said "I guess." They asked me if Todd had found another woman. I said no, it was more like I had found another man. They looked puzzled.

My parents called up my brother George, and my sisters, Marie and Karen. When Karen walked in she said, "Well, I recognize the voice…" George had tears in his eyes.

I soon told everybody about Malcom and how he "loved" me. How he was waiting for me to join him. My beliefs about this "affair" alarmed them. I remember asking my sister, Casey, who lived at the house, what she thought of my professor and our prospects.

She said, "I wouldn't hold my breath."

It didn't take long before I decided that my family knew about Malcom and that they were part of the "information network" working against me. They all had ulterior motives, I concluded. Feeling so, I separated myself from a big family dinner, and took my plate of food outside to eat on the porch swing. Later, one of my brother-in-laws came out to pick up my plate. No words were exchanged.

This set the pattern for any psychotic break I would have in future years. The paranoia about my family "lying to me about Malcom," and then, trying to "keep us apart." They knew everything, and I was convinced they were trying to keep me in Phoenix, away from him.

After formulating a new set of "realizations" about my life, I decided to go into the house and lock myself in the main bathroom. I would meditate to bring forth the truth. On the pretext of wanting her bobby pins, my mother tried to reach me. I wouldn't respond. Different people in my family also tried to talk with me. Finally, I decided to answer one phone call, it was from my former-shrink, brother-in-law, Harold. I thought he might have some answers.

He just said, "Anne, it's been a long time since we've talked. You know you've got your mother worried."

I noticed that he never asked me how I was. I replied, "There's nothing to worry about. I'm doing just fine."

Then, and almost as if trying to reinforce his indifference to that statemnet, he said, "Well, how is your sister Casey, doing?"

"She's fine" I said, with the same reply about Jane.

I then told him, "Here, talk to them yourself, if you want to know how they are, talk to them." and I handed the phone over to someone.

I then went back and again locked myself in the bathroom. Once more, they tried to lure me out. Finally, I came out for my brother, and told him about me and Malcom.

After that, we went into the living room where my parents were. He told them it was a story just like his ex-wife's, where she had found another man and left him due to that. He referred to Malcom as "a guy for Anne from up north." I didn't like his simplistic phrasing of our "serious" love affair. Miffed, I went back out on the porch swing, shunning everyone until I could talk to Malcom.

Around 6:00 p.m., I was still sitting there. I watched Jane bring in a big jar of sun tea. We didn't exchange a word. Soon after that, she and Marie came out to see me along with Marie's three-year-old daughter, Abby. They seemed amused with my behavior, and Abby started yelling, "Talk to me! Talk to me!" I remained silent. Soon after, they went back in the house, from where later I heard the phones ringing over and over.

By the evening of July 20, 1981, my family had everything all set up. I was sitting outside in the dark, with a large stick on the seat, covering any space where someone might attempt to sit. George and Eddie, my sister Marie's husband, came out to take me away.

After turning on a backyard light, and without saying a word, they simply picked me up, each lifting one side, like I was sitting in a chair. They then quickly carried me through the sliding glass door, into the house and outside and into a car heading for the county crisis clinic. Of course, I didn't know that.

Once we arrived at the clinic, I saw my family going into an office in groups. I knew that I was being tested. The "Malcom people" were listening in. I said to George and my sister, Casey, "I will never forgive you for doing this to me. Never." I'll always remember the embarrassed look on my sister's face. I felt a need to be mean to Marie when the doctor finally came for me.

She was crying, saying "Don't make us do this to you...please, Anne!"

I grimaced and replied, for effect, "I can't stand you, get away from me!" I acted that way towards my then favorite sister, thinking to confuse the "Malcom people." I ended with another "I'll never forgive you!" a fitting goodbye from a very "confused" woman.

The doctor, who took me by the arm said, "I hear you've been on a diet?"

"Yes, I used to weigh 135 pounds." I said.

"What is wrong with that?"

Until I was turned over to the male orderlies in the first floor day room, I was still waiting for someone to tell me that it was all a joke. A charade. Just look around.

Instead, the doctor, the orderlies and a nurse escorted me to the women's isolation room. The nurse said, "Please undress and get into this gown." Although I probably would have done that on my own, I was shocked that they expected me to undress in front of all four of them. I hesitated. Angered, the nurse said, in a aggravated voice, "Get her up here!" They pulled me up and across the examining table that was used as a bed. As the nurse gave me a shot of an anti-psychotic drug in my rear, she said, "Oh, she's just a tiny thing." Then they stripped me down, put me in a gown and left after lying me on the table.

I remember the feeling of being left all alone, and isolated, in a place where people are treated so harshly. The ladies bathroom was just outside the isolation room, and anyone could walk in. There was no handle on the door for me to get out, but I somehow got it open.

I walked into the day room off the nurses station. There were just the beginnings of sunlight during that early hour. I pulled my sheet out of the isolation room and walked over to the wide window sill where I draped myself with the sheet. I got groggy. The shot was taking effect and I eventually went to sleep.

I read later that one doctor wrote: "Upon awakening under a sheet, Anne had a 'disarming smile'." That had to have been before I realized where I was. All I had to do to figure that out was to study the other patients in that setting for just five minutes. There were people talking to themselves, rocking back and forth, people staring in a gaze at who knows what, waving over at me as if saying "Welcome to the nut house."

Panicking somewhat, I felt like somebody had made a terrible mistake locking me in with insane people. And was it a result of my family's "conspiracy?" I was sure of it.

The next morning, I was told that my mother had brought some blueberries and clog shoes for me since they had taken away my regular shoes. (Why, I have no idea.) But I was not seeing my family: they were now my "enemies" who lied to get me put in there.

Once I became a client of the county lawyer, hoever, I got to see, firsthand, what the "lies" had been. They would make too much sense to the mental health people who surely thought I needed to be there.

But in retrospect, my family saved me from spending six months at the Arizona State Mental Hospital, which is supposed to be hell compared to county. That was because when discharge time came, I would have a place to go if I had a good attitude towards my family. I guess that's what they were saying. I would be free to go in their charge.

In committing me, my family had had to show that I was harmful to myself or to others. They claimed that I was starving myself during the month-long fast back in my D.C. apartment. That was true in a literal sense, but I was really just waiting to be "rescued."

They said I was hearing voices. This was a playoff from my saying that neighbors out in the front of their house were talking. They were.

I also had laid the stick down next to me on my parents' swing to keep anyone from sitting there. My family turned that into an accusation that I had been "swinging a stick at my three year old niece, Abby." That was not true.

But it helped get me "put away" for all practical purposes. And I would stay at the crisis clinic the next several days dealing with that problem. In retrospect? At least I was alive.

CHAPTER 4

A COUNTY CRISIS

In the day room at the county, all of us patients were "under observation," locked out of our rooms. The nurses were behind a huge window which separated their nurse's station from us. They were taking notes and writing in our charts, getting medicine ready for distribution and so on. Every once and a while one of the nurses or doctors would come and sit next to you and get your reaction at that moment.

The day room had a large window on the east side, and the window sill was very deep, the place where I slept my first night there. And on one end of the sill was a phone for patient use, where we could get and place brief calls. Doesn't sound so bad? It was. There was a feeling of abandonment in that room.

There was a brown vinyl couch right below the TV, which somebody was always sleeping on. The room also had about five gold, orange and yellow highback chairs, among several others, and the floors in the whole place were covered with an ugly grayish linoleum. There were enough tables and chairs for about 25 patients to eat breakfast, lunch, dinner and a late evening snack. The main preoccupation in that room seemed to be eating, smoking and taking medication.

This room had a metal lighter with tiny holes that was mounted on a wall. We all had to hold our cigarettes against the screen, push a button and inhale when it turned red. Much like a cigarette lighter in cars. For those without their own cigarettes, the nurses rationed out hand-rolled ones. It was that long ago.

But while everyone else on the "outside" watched Prince Charles' wedding, I sat there, approached by a man who thought he was Jesus Christ, offering me a hand-rolled cigarette. This was highly unusual for that hospital since most patients asked for cigarettes. I hesitated for a few seconds. Hadn't I given up the habit during the 38-day fast and during the bus ride to Phoenix? Yes I had, and it had not been painless. Now, however, nothing sounded better, except to be out of that "pit," as my father called it. Or to be with my husband, whoever that might be. So, I had my first of many more cigarettes to come.

There was a daily routine some of us followed. Every morning, after a hellish night of fear and uncertainty for me, since I had not yet figured out that most schizophrenics were gentle souls, I would take a shower. That was partly so the doctors would know I was ready to leave.

Then I would have an audience with about five people: two psychiatrists, one psychologist, a counselor and a social worker. They asked "practical" questions, like how we felt that morning, sleepy or wide awake? What did I think about my thoughts, were they strange to me? and so on. It was obvious that I was considered atypical because I wasn't a homeless person, or somebody further "gone," but they were of course willing to send me to the state hospital if anyone in my family had insisted.

But I knew I had to maneuver around the questions, especially, "Can you tell us what brought you here?"

My answer usually consisted of some version of, "My family," and that must not have been what they wanted to hear since they asked me the same thing every time. I got to the point where I said it was my strange ideas about "a professor back east," or that my family was "in on the conspiracy," or I knew how "important" I was, "what a good student I used to be," etc. That sort of response seemed much more acceptable to them.

I really did have a framework with a place for all the delusions to fit into whenever I lost touch with reality. At times, and over the years, the story would take on totally bizarre ideas, such as those you've already heard-among many others.

Almost always the problem was along the lines of: people were talking about me, laughing at me, thinking I'm a phony, thinking I was a "loose woman," etc. They must have thought I'm "immoral and embarrassing" and on and on. But the basic story never changed, there was the Malcom and Anne "romance."

The doctors became aware that the gist of the bizarre notion was that my honors thesis advisor, Malcom Collins, was in love with me. He was waiting for me to rejoin him so we could get on with our love story, something that started on the day he did his presentation on labor economics in front of my "honors seminar" class on Valentine's Day. Of course I managed to find him the following week at the graduate library, wearing his black coat. I took that opportunity to tell him I was going to use his presentation as a basis for one of the papers due in that class. Obviously, I was delusional about the man at that time, having developed this complex and bizarre fantasy.

My lawyer wanted to defend me against the claims that my family had filed against me. He said that I had a good case and that Todd was even going to testify on my behalf. (A lie.) If I had held onto my resolve, though, it would have just been me and Mr. Thomas against my family. If I lost the case, I would be sent to the state mental hospital. I had driven by there many times back in my "normal" days. A dreary looking place, all the patients locked into a big parcel of land by high chain link fences. Like cattle on a ranch. Hard to believe there could be a place worse than the county crisis clinic.

But that was never going to happen. My lawyer showed me that it was not just my family who were going to vote for the asylum for six months, but also my psychiatrists and psychologist. I heard from the social worker that if I would just go "voluntarily" up to the third floor, where the patients weren't as extremely delusional, I would not have to worry about that.

Also, my family told me if I would just <u>admit</u> that I needed to be there, it would never be "in the records" that I had been committed. Of course that was not true. But this seemed like a better idea than fighting the system, so I gave in.

That was very hard for me to do following a certain scene with my mother. I had agreed to talk to my parents while my head was leaning sideways because of the effects of the anti-psychotic drug Haldol. I was sure my parents would want to call the whole thing off after they saw me.

I went into the room and peered sideways into my mother's eyes as I pleaded with her to tell them to release me. All she said was "But Anne, you need 'treatment'." I was devastated by that one-on-one interaction with her. I felt betrayed; that certainly a "mother's unconditional love" was not there for me.

When I talked to my family after my release, they had defended what they had done, claiming there had been no other way to deal with me. As much as I hate to say it, they were probably right.

While these events were happening, I never really had my psychosis under control. Taking Haldol was worse to me than not having any medication at all. I was physically distressed, as I said, with my head bent to the side, my feet tapping and my body rocking slowly back and forth. That the doctors kept giving it to me made it seem like the drug was a punishment. And for what, for being in love? It was upsetting. Later they gave me Cogentin, an anti-Parkinsonian medication, to ease the side-effects of the Haldol. It did.

Reflecting back, I know there are at least 15 different anti-psychotic medications. Why wasn't something else tried? Perhaps indifference? More so since my family had me cared for as an "indigent" instead of contacting Todd, who still had me on his health insurance as his wife.

Gradually, my doctors relented to letting me move out of their domain. The group who seemed like a parole board probably thought that I seemed pretty sane. It worked out that I did go voluntarily to the third floor, being exceedingly positive about the prospect of getting to leave that place for good in a week or two.

My social worker had always said I should talk to my family, so she was glad when I did. The psychologist who had given me a multiple choice test told me that I was just as normal as any person on the street. In retrospect, that wasn't saying much. The second psychiatrist who had wanted to study me longer, gave my lawyer a complete report about my delusions, indicating that I needed much more treatment.

The only person who seemed upset about the move was my lawyer. He was surprised that I would go to the third floor when I had such a "good case." He saw my commitment as coming about through lies and innuendo, just as I had told him. He also said it was against the law for them to have forced me to take Haldol. I went up anyway. Maybe, even in my eyes, I had acted insanely during the fast. That realization might have come through even though my medication wasn't actually correcting the psychosis. But now that things seemed a little better; there was talk about my being released. I was sure I would have to put out a big effort, though, and went up to "three," hoping for the best.

The third floor was not that different from the second. There was a day room, though not as large, and only two patients to a bedroom, rather than three. I thought I would be leaving behind a male friend I had made on the other floor, but he moved up on the same day as me. He wasn't psychotic, but suicidal. Though back then people also thought there was something "abnormal" about him being gay. But it had made me feel safer knowing someone like that. We had had some interesting talks.

My family found my new fellow patients to be almost as entertaining as those on two. Anyone who's seen any of the "insane asylum" types of movies knows exactly what I mean. It made me feel a bit uneasy talking about the other patients, but that's in small part what kept my family coming in. And it made time go by, since often it was hard to make conversation about where I was.

The nurses were saying seven more days, and I thought that was the time limit to finish all the "requirements." One thing I got excited about was the required "autobiography." I spent a lot of time on it, writing about my relationships with my family,

Todd, my childhood, and so on. When the nurse asked for everyone in the group to share their thoughts, I had about eight pages of fairly insightful material.

They also had arts and crafts, and I painted inside the stained glass outlines as best I could. I would rather have not "had to" do it, but it made for less time for me to think about solutions for my unresolved issues.

All along, I was fantasizing about the Malcom Collins puzzle, our getting together being a goal that kept me happy. The Haldol had some effect; I wasn't as obsessed with that to the extent I had been. And all the family togetherness was very positive for my self-esteem, me feeling a little less schizophrenic than before.

But since nothing seemed real to me or my family about my situation anyway, nobody bothered to stop and think what specific ideas I was really thinking about. I was in a place that was so removed from the real world I sometimes felt like that mouse in a maze. Were the mental health people being cynical, using plastic mattresses, taking away shoes, having intermittent flows of water in the shower stalls, etc.?

I was assigned a single psychiatrist on the third floor, a young woman. We had a long conversation, about Todd, about having "fallen in love" with another man, about my goals, etc. The doctor thought I seemed realistic enough to send home. I complained about having to take something for my bent neck syndrome, so she put me on another anti-psychotic drug called Stelazine. Another anti-psychotic drug that never did work 100 percent.

In fact, when I left the county that first time, I hadn't yet figured out what kind of medication kept everyone happy until I looked down at a paper I had to sign. I saw the words: "Type of Medication: anti-psychotic," and "Diagnosis: psychotic break." So that's what they all had been thinking. I would have never come to that conclusion myself since my thoughts seemed so down to earth to me.

Heading home, I was thinking about mundane things, like where to find a job. I was still waiting to get together with Collins at the "appropriate" time as I saw it. But now everybody had to wait until the beginning of the fall semester of 1981 for the plot to thicken. Then Malcom would be teaching, Todd would be working towards his economics Ph.D at Tydings, and I would be ready to come back east to my "proper place" in Malcom's house. (Dear God.)

The Stelazine worked about as well as the Haldol had, minus the side effects. Activity surrounded me then, and I must have seemed cured of my mental illness. My family probably felt they were taking a risk, though, not being able to predict what I might do. My mother, I knew, was thinking about all eight of her children in making her decisions. I knew she was nervous about me, in large part because of a phone call she made to me in the hospital.

"Anne—have you <u>hurt</u> anyone?"

"No, what are you talking about?"

"I just got a call from the police about a man at the bus station downtown."

"No, mom, that was about me getting my purse stolen."

"Oh, thank God…I was worried."

I heard what she said and was aware that I was going to be feared as someone potentially explosive from then on. My mother no doubt felt, after learning about some of the seamier sides of my life, that it was my own behavior entirely that led up to my break from reality. And that might in fact be true. And mentally ill people are supposed to be violent, aren't they? I would run into that prejudice against me many times in the future. Sadly, the first time was from my own mother.

CHAPTER 5

BUCKLING DOWN

At the end of my first stay at the county crisis clinic in July 1981, I made a conscious decision to get a job and remain at my parents' home rather than return to Todd in Washington, D.C. Kind of a boring choice, but with all the strange thoughts in my head, that was understandable. I didn't think about my family as being part of a "conspiracy" like I did before, but I was still thinking about Malcom in one corner of my mind.

But I needed to sift through things and come to terms with what had happened to me. It was rather bizarre that I hadn't seen or heard from Todd for more than a month.

Later I saw some self portraits he had drawn during that painful time which show a expression of horror on his face. He had suggested honors courses as a big gesture I could make at Tydings after getting all those A's back at Matthews University when first returning to college. Did he deserve some of the pain caused by that unfortunate suggestion? Not really.

Heading back to my parents' home after my first hospitalization, it was assumed that I would look for a job. My parents felt that it would be therapeutic if I did, and I had always seen myself as employed back then too, even in spite of my checkered work history.

In summer 1981 my sister Casey was home for the summer, and she worked to save up money for her school year in Georgia. She got me a job in an office downtown as a clerk, which was such a letdown after getting a college degree. But I had forgotten so much factual information during the fast, an experience I still couldn't fathom. In any case, I didn't do that well at the job.

Even though I drove with Casey to and from work every weekday, it became a depressing ride for me. She was very optimistic and always interesting, but I still ended up predictably unhappy with my job. But life went on, and I fulfilled my responsibilities. It was very tedious, and I felt like I was doing time.

I was vacuous as usual, which was more or less the tendency I had since the ground zero situation at Tydings. And as I've said, I had forgotten so much, especially when it came to having to learn anything complicated. But the job made time go by, and I assumed this was my role for the present. Todd was busy in D.C., with what, I didn't know.

In between this drudgery, I went to see a "psychotherapist" at a clinic near my parents' home. Ominously, this turned out to be a foreshadowing of what would happen again and again with me and psychologists. The ones I saw just weren't very professional. As I listened to the woman's theories about me and Malcom Collins, I realized that there was something there "between us," even though the Stelazine was at least partially effective. If this woman could see it, then it must be real. Of course I would think that.

It was similar to the situation I had with a psychology Ph.D candidate earlier during my last semester at Tydings University in fall 1980. He audio taped me once a week, even shared it with one of the psychology professors, and they never realized that I was delusional and that the story I had to tell wasn't quite true. They too needed some schooling in how to recognize psychosis when confronted with it.

In August 1981, one month after my first committment, I told yet another psychologist about Malcom, and once again, she assumed that the professor and I had actually had an affair and that he could be "scared to see me again." Again, there was something missing. Ultimately, these sessions further confused my highly developed fantasy about the whole Tydings experience. In 1998, I changed my mind about psychologists because I found a very good one to talk to. She is insightful and is good at dealing with me as a paranoid schizophrenic. There's really a new "practical" approach to people like me. Not "What made you feel that?" but "What can you do about it?" She was never "shocked" by anything I said and was a very intelligent person.

Even though I was becoming increasingly depressed with my job, I kept busy. Once, when my boss asked me out to lunch, I read all sorts of motives into his offer. Later, my relatively sane side decided to quit taking the anti-psychotic medication. I reasoned that Malcom would resent the implication that what I thought about the two of us wasn't real.

Over the years, gradually, I found out that it took about three or four weeks for the delusions to return in full force after I stopped taking the medication. Of course there was all that time at the beginning of my illness in 1980 when I was on no medication at all for over a year when I should have been on it. That caused the most harm to my brain.

But in fall of 1981, after stopping my "meds," trivial things started to become "significant" again. For example, Casey had lent me her "Preppy Handbook" to read. It all seemed so wholesome, and I thought of myself as a preppy. Of course I surmised that Malcom must consider himself one too. To the untrained eye, I was acting "normally." Clinically, I was getting closer and closer to a second psychotic break. Not being on anti-psychotic medicine was not a good idea.

Eventually, I viewed my job at the water resources office as a farce. I felt that once again the "wool was being pulled over my eyes." I realized that even my boss and co-workers at ICC, where I had gotten a job right after graduation, had also been part of the ruse. I felt betrayed.

In defiance, I went out to the back porch swing at my parents' home, and layed down. I knew that my mom kept looking through Casey's back window to check on me. They were probably a litle scared. Fortunately, I never got violent in any of my psychotic breaks towards anyone. That would have changed everything. Then I'd definitely have been put at the state mental hospital. And that would have confirmed the prejudice of many people towards people with mental illness. But I learned quickly that we are not all violent.

As soon as I surmised that my whole family was again trying to keep me and Malcom apart, I began another downward slide from reality. Why would they be plotting against me was something I ignored. Maybe I was also stupid? That's probably what some people would say. But there I was on a porch swing, pretending to be asleep when I really wasn't. For what reason I don't remember. Maybe for the shock value.

The next morning, around 7:00 a.m., my mother came out and asked me why I wasn't getting ready for work. I told her I couldn't work," that I must be a conventional "housewife" at Collins' and my house. My mother sighed and went inside. She came back shortly afterwards and sat beside me on the swing. She encouraged me to tell her what I was thinking. I agreed, only if she promised never to take me back to the county hospital. She promised me that she wouldn't.

I felt safe for a few minutes and talked to her about what had been going on, including a little about Malcom. I even asked her why she had read Todd's letters to me. She said she felt she had to. Although angry, I was at least happy that she was being honest. I watched from the porch swing as she walked away, though, and wondered if she really could be trusted.

Several hours passed with lots of phone calls coming in. My dad came out to hand me half of his Big Apple barbecued beef sandwich. I grudgingly grabbed it from him and wolfed it down. Who did I think I was? At dinner time he brought out a plate of homemade spaghetti, which I decided not to eat. I was lucky that I had such nice people waiting on me. But by then, I again had decided not to talk to anyone.

My father came out again and said angrily, "You tricked that psychiatrist into letting you out!" I started to get nervous. Then Roy, married to one of my cousins, came out and tried to get me to talk, to no avail. Finally, he and my father came out and each took one arm of mine and pulled me through the house and into the car.

While holding my hand in the back seat, my father told me that "Everything is going to be OK." It wasn't far to the Maryvale clinic where I had seen the psychologist recently. Instead of going into her office, though, they took me in to see the psychiatrist.

I wouldn't talk, in spite of Roy explaining that "Her husband back in Washington, D.C. wants her to come back." During this ordeal I was dragged around by my arms while I was barefoot. The woman psychiatrist decided that I should go back into the county crisis clinic and promised to make the necessary calls. Later, at the reception desk inside the clinic, I began to cry softly about my mother's broken promise.

Roy told the "white coat" who came to get me, "She's psychotic, but not assaultive." He was a policeman back east in Lawrence. I was escorted down the hall, and once inside the locked ward, was handed over to an orderly who showed me into the isolation room.

I asked him if I could use the phone, and he agreed. I actually dialed Washington, D.C. information from the day room. The operator said there was no listing for a "Malcom Collins" there. I knew then that Roy had been lying about "her husband in Washington, D.C." I was being overly literal.

So I sat there in the day room feeling terribly depressed. A nurse came up to me with some Stelazine, which I had stopped taking about three weeks before. I refused it and just sat there by the phone. The nurse called the orderlies over who each took me by the arm. I stood up, but scared, I pulled back a little with my weight.

One of the orderlies said, "OK, if that's how you want it," and proceeded to bulldoze me back into the isolation room. They asked me to get up on the examining table. I hesitated once again. So they forcibly got me on my back and tied up both of my arms with leather restraints. That shocked and angered me, and I decided it was all a test to see how determined I could be. This time the nurse came in with a hypodermic and stuck me in my right thigh. It was at that point that I made a conscious decision not to speak to anyone or eat anything until my "husband" rescued me.

CHAPTER 6

FINALLY RESCUED

How could the people at the county crisis clinic have forgotten what a non-imposing and gentle person I was when I stayed there for almost two weeks just a few months before? I was furious, and felt violated and humiliated. I did nothing but stare at the ceiling and cringe every time a nurse came in with a shot.

I managed to fall asleep on my back, and woke up the next morning when I heard my father trying to make me drink some milk. I purposely let it fall on the floor. Since I wouldn't eat, the hospital staff forced a tube feeder down my nose. That was a painful procedure, forcing the thick plastic tube to bend at the back of my throat. I thought it was all too complex the way everybody was handling their "roles." I just wished we could all open up and communicate with each other honestly.

They seemed determined to make me talk; people would come in alone or in pairs. The latter were more interesting, since I got to hear discussions about me as if I weren't there. I cringed at the thought of talking to any of my family or to the "professionals" treating me. I was not speaking to anyone, because whoever "they" were, they obviously did not have my best interests at heart. Certainly not with me strapped to a table like that.

Some relief in the whole melodrama came when I heard that my husband was coming to see me. I was so excited; I knew my ordeal would be over soon. Good thing they were using the word "husband" when mentioning the visit, or Todd would also have gotten the silent treatment. I was definitely interested in seeing my husband, even if I wasn't quite sure who it would be.

While staring rigidly at the ceiling, I felt a breeze as another person walked in. Out of the blue, I heard my name, "Anne" as he caught sight of me. I recognized the sound of that voice immediately.

"Todd," I said, and tried to get up, forgetting for a moment the restraints on my arms. It was such a relief to finally know who was who. The orderlies untied me and I got up and hugged Todd very hard. Here was someone I really wanted to see. We had spent so much time together that a lot of feelings went unspoken. It was like starting over after all we had been through. The two of us went into the day room to talk. My mother was there too. A bizarre aspect of those memorable moments was that while I was sitting in a chair and talking, I still had the tube feeder on my face and down my throat. What a sight I must have been. Unbelievably, I didn't feel self-conscious, and Todd and my mother acted as if nothing were wrong.

A lighter moment came while we were sitting at a table, and a female patient started writhing on the floor, screaming and calling herself a "whore." I looked at them and said, "There's somebody getting 'treatment'." My mother laughed a little, got up and kissed her strange daughter on the forehead and left.

I wished that Todd and I could just get up and run away together. But he had been briefed about me and my case, and was worried about how to act around me. My mental condition was only partially stabilized—just a half hour earlier to be exact. Even while I was still being given shots during my silence, I found out later that my determination had been labeled "catatonia," and if I hadn't started communicating, would have received shock treatments the next day. Hearing this, my family had finally summoned Todd.

He told me about new arrangements that were being made for me. They involved being transferred to a private hospital, Belair, and being assigned to a new psychiatrist. I agreed to be admitted there after another audience with the medical team. Commenting about Belair, I told them that I thought it would just be another day room to sit in. With that they let me go.

On my first night at Belair, I was put in the locked ward. But was it really locked? I didn't know. Although there was no smoking inside, it was a beautiful night in October for me and Todd to go outside to smoke. There were two beds to a room with plain mattresses (at the county, they were coated with heavy plastic). That made it seem a lot nicer. In addition there was a normal shower compared to the county's intermittent flow of water that stopped every few minutes so you couldn't drown yourself.

The morning after my arrival, I met my new psychiatrist. He was an older, burly man with a very brisk way of speaking, as if I was an intrusion. His first comment, upon seeing me, was that I seemed a lot healthier than described: "catatonic patient refusing to speak or eat." Presumably, he was chosen as my psychiatrist because of his familiarity with shock treatment, just in case he needed to use it.

That first meeting lasted about fifteen minutes, a far cry from the "team of professionals" at the county on each case, who lined up mornings like an audience at a play. Looking back at that, though, that arrangement did seem like a good effort by them for each individual patient. One thing I wasn't sure about with the county clinic, though, was whether they did that much for every patient.

Similar to that team at the county was what Belair called "psycho-drama," where patients played out their neuroses or anxieties in front of their peers and therapists. About 35 people in all. Then there was me, armed with my delusions about Malcom and my daring decision to get up there and do a "skit" of my own. The man playing "Collins" told me to "Go away and quit bothering me."

It upset me, but the skit ended and I returned to my seat. Afterwards, at the outdoor lounging area, some of the patients asked me when I had had the affair. They couldn't believe, after having seen my acting, that Collins and I had never been lovers. And I could barely believe I gave that performance. In any case, it was clear to them then that I really was psychotic, an outsider in a group of people with mainly common psychological symptoms.

Advice started filtering through from my fellow patients that I was very lucky to have a husband as nice as Todd. They said he must be very kind and understanding. In another group session, other female patients, manic depressives, people with depression, anxiety, etc. tried to talk me into giving Todd another chance. Actually, it should have been the other way around, but back in 1981, I was the one with more authority.

It was an uncanny situation being at a hospital for mental illness, where the sick were not really physically impaired. Lacking the more common inquiries about pain, it created an air of tension between patients and visitors. One time while playing a card game called "45" with my parents and Todd, I remember saying something sarcastic to my mother about my hospitalizations. She seemed momentarily alarmed. I think back then she was probably always thinking there was a chance I could get violent.

In all, it seemed that I and the few schizophrenics at Belair got to entertain the more "normal" patients and their visitors, a reversal of attitudes in what I experienced at the county.

Todd took a more serious stance in all this mental hospital business. He knew that I had gotten some help with my problems, but felt that what he witnessed in his short time at the county was uncalled for. Eventually, it came time for him to go back to his job and to our home in Washington, D.C. Although he tried to convince me that our fates were interwoven, I was still muddled due to the drug Stelazine and maintained a "let's be friends" attitude regarding our marriage.

We hugged, and Todd, though looking somewhat dejected, left with a tenuous peace of mind that things would work out. I dealt with my mild confusion about our marriage by going to the arts and crafts center to paint some vases. I no longer thought that Malcom was my husband, one positive aspect of my stay at Belair. Still, I wondered who I would end up with.

After what went on the afternoon before Todd left, the advice about "Hey Anne, get real. He's a great guy." I realized that I was wasting my time at Belair. I left the crafts center to try to get a hold of Todd before he flew back east. At that point, I was not interested in anything else. As I squeezed my way through a crowd gathering for a performance, I looked up and saw Todd looking for <u>me</u>. I felt as happy as I had when he came to my rescue while I was strapped down at the crisis clinic. We embraced after talking very briefly.

He had just been to see the movie "Arthur" about the drunk millionaire, and had decided to try and get me back one more time. He still left town, but now there was hope about us and our marriage, though the details were still sketchy. Soon after, I was released to go home with my parents. As I found things pretty dull there, the time was ripe for a big change.

I kept a follow-up appointment with my Belair Hospital psychiatrist a few days after I returned home. He started discussing my personality, how I was so strong in contrast to Todd's passive personality. He mentioned how bored I might be in a relationship like that. He was amazed when I said I was thinking about rejoining Todd back east. Had he been out of touch? I wondered. He quickly changed his tune, and said "I would not discourage you from doing that."

After that appointment, I decided to get out of Phoenix. My destiny, I felt, was to go back to D.C., to be with either Malcom or Todd. I called my sister, Marie with a strange request. I had Malcom's correct phone number and asked her to call him at home and find out where he stood in regards to our "relationship." After phoning him, she called me to explain that a woman had answered and was angry that somebody would try to reach him at night like that.

At that point, I realized that there was another woman in Collins' life and that it was time for me to move on. In later psychotic breaks, I would look back at that call Marie had made and decide that she had lied about the whole thing. Ungraciously, and in that time frame of October 1981, I was ready to try and make my marriage to Todd a successful one, even if he had been my second choice. But of course the Malcom idea was obviously all in my head.

I didn't leave much time for the news about the professor to sink in. Again, it was similar to my feeling at getting rescued at the county. I was happy and relieved. With much self-confidence and in a wonderful state of mind, I dialed our townhouse in D.C. "Hi Todd, it's me. Do you still want me back? I know we can work things out."

Todd said "Yes, of course," and we talked very cheerfully and briefly about my flying back once he wired the money. He later told me that his mother and brother were there at that time and told him they couldn't believe he would take me back. Not a big surprise.

On the day of my flight to Washington, D.C., I said goodbye to whoever was around. My family was relieved that things had worked out for me so I could resume a "normal" life back with my husband. It was a night flight, and about four hours after taking off from Phoenix, I once again saw the familiar monuments and the rivers. As the plane landed, I got off and there was Todd, looking dapper and happy. A big hug and a kiss ensued, and then we went to a restaurant in Old Towne, Alexandria, for some tiger shrimp and beer.

I was happy with Todd, and was feeling good to have put my mental illness behind me. And my condition could have been just a short-term ordeal, though I was still somewhat confused. As I talked to Todd, we knew what had happened twice before could happen again. My Belair doctor had explained that since I had become delusional again after stopping the anti-psychotic medication, I must be considered a true schizophrenic.

Despite that fact, Todd and I had a talk. By the time we were almost back to our townhouse, Todd knew that I was no longer on birth control pills. We hadn't yet thought about how important having a baby would become to us. And we hadn't discussed the fact that he or she would have about a 12 percent chance of inheriting my mental illness. For the moment, I was happy about being home with Todd again. The reality of my "purge" had not sunk in yet.

CHAPTER 7

ON THE BRINK

My problem with worrying about things I couldn't change didn't blossom until I returned to Matthews University as a 26-year-old sophmore in September 1978. None of this mental illness stuff was even vaguely in my mind before then. That I would one day end up evolving into a schizophrenic? I would have laughed.

And I was yet to be truly "aware" that I had thrown all my belongings away in that unfortunate summer of 1981 until I flew back to D.C. to be with Todd in October of that same year. Being alone those six months in Phoenix didn't count, since I could not look at my empty study room and see for myself what was actually gone. And what was missing was a lot; my great corduroy couch, my irreplacable study table, and of course especially all of my books and notes, among other things.

But there were other things to face. When I went back to D.C., I had so far failed in the one job I got after Tydings and the one clerical job I secured through Casey in downtown Phoenix. Add to that a gutted shell for a "study room," and there were a lot of negative things going on.

Back in 1977-78 I had gotten to the point in my life where I wanted to get that bachelor's degree, partly because people were driving me nuts calling me "support staff" due to my not having one. Which probably shouldn't have fazed me. But by 1977 and 1978 I was already focused on excelling in school. I knew that if the "assistant to the director" could do it, then I could too.

My not being satisfied with my life's activities happened at the same time as my having a good job during 1977 and 1978. Unusual for me. But both Todd and I seemed to come to the conclusion together: I would be a "returning" student back at Matthews University in Phoenix.

Todd also had wanderlust. Tired of his job with the federal government, he wanted to explore "solar energy" in a place where it made sense—the desert in Arizona. That neither of us had thought through whether we were on the right track was not important. In our thinking, such details were seemingly unimportant, something that we didn't care to have a logical conclusion for. How were we going to live? Presumedly off of our savings. Out-of-state tuition? So what.

I knew what I needed to do to become a sophmore at Matthews; it involved making a trip out to Phoenix to pre-register in late spring 1978. I had already become a control freak. So with Todd and me using our heads together, we had ended up with me being perfectly ready to be taught by just the right teachers and professors at the right time.

Todd had a lot of experience at Matthews taking and enjoying classes. Should I also take "labor economics" from professor Brown? Todd had enjoyed it, and that was good enough for me. I wanted to "maximize my utility" way before I ever found out what that meant. According to Todd, that is still the situation in life for me. He says I only do what I want for myself and the people around me. But Todd and I were both aware that our lives needed to be prioritized before any more big decisions were going to be made. What had happened to me had been big: I had become psychotic. Over 99 percent of the U.S. population never had anything like that happen. In a way, Todd had probably not yet fully recovered from the shock of seeing me strapped down to a table with a tube feeder through my nose in an isolation room at the county.

My returning to our townhouse which I hadn't seen for over six months made me feel strange. Todd had changed things around, with a new leather chair and some lighting fixtures that looked all shiny and impressive. But as I said, it still was the place with my study room gutted from my move to the apartment. There was nothing left but two black chairs and the white plastic bookshelves in a room that now was just a shell of itself, as they say.

I was shocked to see the stark reality of the outcome of my unfortunate purge. It wasn't something I could take back. Everything was gone, except for the albums and pictures. Luckily, I hadn't taken any of that with me for the move. But within a few weeks, the first signs of my approaching depression started up.

There was more for me to face up to. Todd had always wanted me to work, and late 1981 was no exception, despite my recent history. Back then it was something that I didn't question. So I wasn't home but for a few days when I went to an employment agency in the same building as the consulting firm I got fired from about six months before. Embarrassingly, I ran into my former supervisor. Last time he had seen me I was refusing to talk to him or anyone else at the firm. That very efficient group of people had very efficiently got me out of that office three months after I had started working there right out of college.

Desperate about a job, I asked him if I could ever come back and he said, "There are no openings, though you were pretty good at organizing files." As I've said, the truth is that when I had started and left there my memory of the facts I had learned at college were mostly a blur. It was as if the long curse of the schizophrenia had slowly blocked a lot of my memories about "facts." I could still interview well, but God help me if you ask me about "dummy variables" or anything technical like that.

That very day at the agency I had a possible employer to go to for an interview after taking a typing test. They had told me not to write or say anything about being fired six months before by the consulting firm. In fact they didn't even have me include it in my application. Thus, the lying about my mental illness began.

Mr. Cunningham, the man who interviewed me, had a very harsh nature and was trying to be nice in spite of it. I nodded a lot, especially when he stressed that he preferred getting somebody with a degree and that my former employer (skipping to before the group of statisticians) had raved about me. Little did they know. However, he must have liked my reserved and quiet nature that day, which was really my melancholy due to being there. So I was hired as a secretary once again.

Soon after, I noticed my moodiness about the new job. It didn't help that Todd, afraid I would throw everything out again, had me buy all my clothes at a nearby <u>Goodwill</u> store. I ended up with shiny paisley dresses that made me self-conscious since the other employees all dressed well. This situation coming about after my having read my sister Casey's "Preppy Handbook" made it all the worse.

The disarray of that time was a period in my life I later needed to put aside for the sake of sanity. And I also made myself forget what an ogre Todd had been with Goodwill stores and all.

A part of the job that I disliked so much was sitting directly in front of two men, one of them being my boss, Mr. Cunningham. He bragged to Todd once that he liked to be able to "just snap my fingers and my girl gets the proper file." I also had to be trained in how to deal with contracts and proposals and master a big filing system. However, I could not and would not learn their system—it confused me. And I had become so depressed it affected my life even at home.

Upon sensing a dissatisfaction from others about my work, I decided to talk to my boss and the two women who were training me, telling them that "I had become psychotic and had been in love with this professor." I also pointed out that I knew I wasn't doing well at my job, even that I had lied about getting fired. Also, that I was taking an anti-psychotic medication that was causing my confusion and that I was going to "clear my head" by stopping taking it. They asked if that was wise, and told me, no doubt untruthfully, that they would keep my secret between the four of us.

A few days later, I started receiving very strange assignments, like alphabetizing all the files in certain boxes on Saturdays so there wouldn't be a mess for the other employees to work around. I even did it once a few weeks later. By that particular Saturday morning, I had become very agitated and was having strange thoughts about the two men who during the week sat directly across from me. I saw one of them on that Saturday and was so nervous that I got sick.

I even decided to go home rather than pick up Todd from work a few miles away. He too decided to do a Saturday along with me, and I was just so mixed up in my mind that I pictured that people were still "testing" me. So once again Todd got stuck without a ride home. My paranoia was rampant, and the Stelazine was only partially working to keep my mind straight. Such chaos. Eventually that day, Todd and I were back at home together, and he wasn't as mad at me as he probably should have been for leaving him stranded.

On the day I actually resigned, I went up to the "sick room" on the second floor and chain-smoked, putting cigarettes out on the wallpaper. Then they claimed it was because I didn't give two week's notice that I was denied severance pay. I was angry, but what I had done had also been very tacky.

An amazing part of all this was Todd's and his parents' attitudes about me and that job. I virtually cried in front of them on a few occasions about how much I hated that job, especially after I had told my supervisors that I was a schizophrenic. And my feelings were not just a flippant disdain; I was extremely depressed. They felt that they were "liberals," but my life should have seemed worth more than some idea about employment. They thought I might be better off if I was "occupied" with a job. I just tell myself that they didn't fully understand my state of mind.

I really didn't talk much to anyone about my confusion then, in the winter of 1981, when I believed that one of the men across from me thought that I was "hitting on him." This was an example of some leftover paranoia following the Malcom Collins experience, when I thought others might believe that I could be a "loose woman." That had happened too at the research firm right after Tydings.

I discount the time between the second commitment and getting back on an effective anti-psychotic in February 1982, as a psychotic time. However, I did have some confusion and delusions mixed in with the overriding depression I was suffering from. In fact, I became so nervous that Todd hid the steak knives and other sharp instruments from me, fearing that I might take my own life.

Todd had eventually told me, "Either you come with me to get help or I'll leave." Not much later, I started seeing a psychiatrist once a week, with Todd going along to make sure they took me seriously. I had thought that I could stop taking all anti-psychotics, but I couldn't.

We decided to go to a mental health clinic in Wheaton, Maryland. There they met with an "intake officer" who took down our story before calling her supervisor. Once again, mine was an unusual case. Most people who have become psychotic don't simply walk into a clinic with their sane spouses. Generally, psychiatrists first perceive the condition in a hospital.

The first psychiatrist they had me talk to alone asked ridiculous questions, and I didn't let him get away with it. I answered, "Of course I'm still Anne—how ridiculous." He also asked what does the saying mean that, "People who live in glass houses shouldn't throw stones." I said I had also heard the one about "A rolling stone gathers no moss." This was the type of inaneness I encountered in my many visits with psychiatrists. I actually only wanted to know if he could help me find a job, that I had to get a job. He must know how difficult it would be for me. "Please help," I implored. "Don't you know of anything?"

I never saw that psychiatrist again.

Next they had me see a psychologist. Todd came along, but it was such a disappointment. I spoke to her with some disregard since the last time I saw a social worker type like that was the summer of 1981, when the woman in Phoenix had told me that Malcom Collins was very upset about our affair and was avoiding me. Todd was there too and listened while I whined about having thrown everything away and of being on the wrong medicine. Todd said he just wanted the psychologist to know that I was telling the truth, which in retrospect was a good idea.

Finally, I ended up in a psychiatrist's office who was supposed to become my "shrink." Again, Todd attended the session, while I told my story and he backed me up. All three of us shared the floor. At the end of the session, Dr. Crow mentioned that he liked the way it had turned out and invited Todd to come next time. The doctor then let me select an anti-psychotic drug from a list of about five. I liked the positive sound of the one called Prolixin, and he put me on 5 mg. per day.

Once I was stabilized with that new drug, it was a little like a social hour with the three of us at Dr. Crow's office every Saturday. He would use my illness as the basis for the conversations, but would also talk to Todd about how he was, and discussed schizophrenia in general. He kept close track of both of us, and you could tell he was fascinated by our "case."

Unfortunately, he was inclined to think for at least seven months that I was a manic-depressive. He told me that a whole new world might open up to me if I tried Lithium, that it was something for us to seriously consider. The closest I could pin him down about schizophrenia was when he said I might have "schizoaffective disorder." He strongly disagreed with the former label calling me a "paranoid schizophrenic." I forget for what reason.

I had read an interesting book that included discussions about the onset of schizophrenia as a basis for determining whether one's illness had a good prognosis or not. The longer the buildup, the worse. The three of us discussed that at one point, and I had some definite ideas.

One example was my seclusive activity while I lived alone for nine months in downtown Milwaukee-late 1971 until June 1972-which I felt was an indication that I was not quite right. But in reality, that move was just a lonely bid to win an old boyfriend back because I thought he would miss me. There was also my desire to get out of my whirlwind of activity in Phoenix at that time, as I've said before. Plus, of course, something in me must have wanted to be a hermit while I lived in that midwest city.

After having lived with me for eight years before my mental breakdown, Todd had a very strong opinion about the onset of my mental illness. He said it was the alcohol that most influenced my schizophrenia, or at least that it played a definite role. And we both knew that the alcoholism itself started at the end of 1975 when the paper packagers went out on strike and I adopted that as a cause.

I had drunk a lot prior, even a bottle of wine each day starting about a year before I met Todd, but my alcoholism didn't start until that strike in 1975, when the cases of cold beer started coming in to strike headquarters. That mixture of friendship, free time and booze was a boiling pot for my alcoholism to brew in. So I suppose alcohol was something that Todd, James, Karl and I were so into that we couldn't tell I was going overboard. Those times were some of the "golden days" of our early 20's. But I was mostly just having fun without doing much thinking.

On the other hand, there was another huge factor in my eventual breakdown—the ludicrous stress I put on myself when returning to college after seven years away. It wasn't long after the association job with the vodka-drinking boss in 1978 that Todd and I had packed up our stuff in D.C. and moved back to Arizona for me to go back to Matthews University starting in the fall.

Since pressure is not always a good thing, one question is why would I decide to choose an overly stressful life, to make a point of pushing too far? Was it for the challenge or my insecurity, or maybe it's something like a gambling addict would do who was hoping his efforts would pay off. I don't know. But it was absurd trying to prove that I could be the "high A" in every class. In reality I was probably just memorizing facts. Nothing of note at all.

It was a pointless goal, and it would lead to its own unnecessary consequence-an eventual nervous breakdown. This for a rolled up diploma and the lifelong memories of my inexplicable race through college. It certainly does not show that I was some high intellect, and why I pushed myself so hard was something I can't really explain to this day.

Psychiatrists would have their own take on that question of why, I'm sure. Maybe they would say there was an unconscious desire on my part to need some type of rescue. Stress being called up and invited in by no one else but me. Who knows? Or maybe I had such low self-esteem that I didn't think I deserved to easily get a degree.

I never really thought much about whether I was trying to compete with Todd in all his laurels. Success did seem to come much more easily for him than me. To give him credit, he was an expert in a lot of things, spending much of his time at work when I wasn't. But I became a completely organized person when I returned to college. I couldn't let it slip by me again. Todd and I were just into different things for a while back then. But the difference ended up making us much closer in our 40's.

But Todd feels I was a sitting duck, so easy to fool because I was too obsessed with the world of university life—or "academia"—for an undergraduate student. And especially for a 26-year-old transfer student returning as a sophmore/junior trying to be a "hot shot" student. Competing with 19- and 20-year-old students straight out of high school was an ultimate challenge, but I didn't mind because I was too oblivious to reality outside of birdogging a good report card.

Todd was there for it all, he had even been the one who had encouraged me to go into the honors program later at Tydings University. I think he still feels a little bit guilty about that. Of course he had nothing to do with the fact that when I returned to school I was on the brink of a personal catastrophe. That turn only showed up at Matthews University in 1978-79 as an extreme case of determination thrown in with a flirtation with an economics professor we both knew: The unlucky Professor Brown. It was fortunate for him that the employment picture never panned out for Todd during those two semesters when I was there. He got to just forward me on the wherever else I was going. Let them deal with the "problem."

CHAPTER 8

FINDING MY NICHE

There was one friend in fall 1980 who said about the D.C. professor at the heart of this book, "Keep far away from that guy." But it was late in the game by that time, and how could I let anybody run me out of the university on a rail? You're different and we don't want you associated with our school? I guess I was supposed to be cognizant of that opinion among some of the academics. I just didn't fit in.

They've undoubtedly heard by now how unfavorable an example I was for the university. I had tried to represent the best of that university in the jobs I've gotten using their credentials. And then I turn around and fail miserably. So many times, and almost all of the exits out of jobs were embarrassing, probably changing the way at least a few firms did their hiring.

Starting my junior year in D.C. in 1979 was fun but hard, just like Matthews. But Tydings was a beautiful microcosm. And after I bragged about how I only got one B out of 12 classes the year before, the director of undergraduate studies in economics wanted to challenge me and show that getting A's there was even harder.

So I later felt that the economics professors at Tydings had set me up from the beginning. Why they would want to I don't know. But I can say, as a full-fledged paranoid person, things were never really above-board for me at Tydings. If I could only have stayed in the background. But I joined the "battle" for good grades, whether it was real or not.

I suppose the effort was for some lofty thoughts about "graduate school." Pretty baffling that my life at that time had lead to this college fantasy. Twenty seven, 28, well these are usually nice ages to be, and I let as little as possible distract me from enjoying myself at whatever I did at those ages, like most young people do. Just one tiny snag—I became a schizophrenic in the process.

But I've often rebelled against overblown times by simply packing my bags and moving away, sometimes literally, sometimes not. In essence I choose the race and then I turn around and reject the prize. College and the whole world of academia was like that for me. Go back and be a marketing major was how I felt when returning in 1978. Fat chance was the ultimate answer. I grew to strongly dislike that subject and the professor teaching it. It was one of those classes where the professor had written the book. Though that can sometimes work out.

Of course I could not automatically tell when I was choosing the riskiest scheme. College had sounded rather inconsequential when I advanced at high school in my senior year. I didn't bother much with the idea of it and had applied to Matthews University just to show my high school counselor that I had applied somewhere. She had insisted. She also had me cut out some of the school newspaper articles that I had written and lay them out nicely under clear plastic in a notebook for an interview at a local radio station. Who knows why she gave me that much effort, but I accepted it. Maybe it was because she was frustrated at my lack of interest. And maybe I did what she said because unconsciously I didn't want the workaday world to start that soon in my life.

But actually I had so ignored the idea of college that I had let go of the college preparatory schedule at the end of my junior year in high school and instead chose a two-semester "secretarial block" rather than physics and calculus for my senior year. I felt that studying and being active at the school was basically enough to have done to go out and get myself a good paying job. A far cry from later stressing out over grades for no type of real job-related goal.

My parents had often said, you could make just as much money at many jobs as somebody with a Ph.D. We were never encouraged to go to college, probably because they just couldn't afford it. That plus I never really studied in high school, just breezing by without much effort.

So it wasn't until after my interview with the radio station in Phoenix that I even thought about moving up the educational ladder. And I didn't know back then how academia could blow over the less serious student. Or the less outgoing student. Or the kids with mental illness.

And by the way, who <u>was</u> minding the store later in my senior year at Tydings? People must have been watching some well-known professor consult with me about my supposed "thesis" every weekday for an hour in that summer farce in 1980? That's what my life became. How to explain how I fit in at this particular time? I was some undergraduate student being given all of that attention from some big shot professor. This time I was impressed by myself—thinking I was something I wasn't.

Who knows if I even would have chosen a university over a community or technical college before ever sitting in that chair beside Collins' desk. Or if I would ever haven gone into college at all. Here I was at a top rated school being engaged as somebody important, and it didn't make sense. It all made me feel appreciated, but the question of why? was still out there as I advanced toward my degree. Little did I know early on that my self-absorption was entertaining to some of the people there at Tydings, and my reaction towards what was happening to me showed how predictable I was.

Sad but true there was really no soothing my insecurity. You must remember that through all of this I was still trying to be the "top A" in my classes. That I had turned around about 180 degrees since the 1970-71 school year in facing a return situation was insignificant to me.

But I told the tape recorder my story at the end of high school in May in 1970. I was giving the interview "in absentia" because my graduation was on the night of the group interview. I said I had wanted to be a writer since 6th grade when I wrote about Jackie Kennedy. It was probably obvious that a Catholic school girl was impressed with her since she became so famous after the assassination. Of course I wanted to continue my education. Where? Matthews University. Just like somebody would expect from a student with good grades and an overabundance of extracurricular activities.

Then about one month after my taped interview, almost in spite of myself, I was chosen as the recipient of the scholarship to Matthews, supposedly to major in journalism. So I went ahead and signed up for journalism 101. However, I dropped out of that rat race about a week after classes began. The class was in some crowded room, and I didn't want to have to compete for articles or to be in somebody's face to get a breaking story or a sound bite. I was probably too lazy for that. But the station still let me have the tuition money, so there was no problem there. And I then became an English major.

But before ever going into the university, I had obtained a job with the telephone company the summer following high school. I had started promptly in June 1970. They had asked me why I didn't want to go to college, and I said I wanted a career with their company instead. And I'm pretty sure I meant it at the time. And they liked me.

So I was assigned to working in the office of the engineers with all of their blueprints spread over their desks. I found it almost amusing that the job actually involved using the shorthand I had learned during my senior year in high school. This was way before I started thinking about situations as being "good karma" or not—those little or big things that happen so on cue as to seem oddly symbolic.

There I was using a practical skill. Little did I realize that in college a lot of everything you learn in high school gets applied to your efforts. Maybe only subtley, but especially with reading and the understanding that comes from reading a lot. So the real stress I experienced came with college. Dear God, everything had been so easy before that. College life was more work than housework and cooking for my family had been, and big mistakes could be made that actually showed up on your report card, like withdrawing from one class or withdrawing from them all, as I did towards the end of my third semester at Matthews when I was 19 years old.

I was taking six courses in fall 1971 when I decided to back out as uneventfully as possible. The academic advisors had me come in for counseling, they did not want me to go. Unlike life later at Tydings U., the people at Matthews liked me being there, even in my first three semesters when I was acting like a nitwit just skimming by. What a difference between my first Matthews party days in 1970-71 to the Matthews obsession days in 1978-79. It was also unfortunate that I had to lose 15 credit hours.

I had learned a good lesson during my "returning to college" days, the way to get good grades was to take good notes. My reasoning was that professors usually have big egos, and they sense that it's only them who can tell the students what they really need to learn. And it worked like a charm for me. I recommend it to my son in high school, but he totally ignores me. And you know, it's something I couldn't explain fully even today to my 18-year-old son. Be careful with grades. You can't let them be so important to you that you obsess over them, but you also can't skip classes and let your grades slide.

What a committment it is when you sign on with a university or probably even a community college. Your record is there, always there. I might as well admit that a lot of what I did with my life showed up in one way or another on my academic record.

In fact, a very confusing time frame was that sophmore year in college when I decided to drop out. The reasons for doing that were subdued compared to my just needing to blow off my hometown of Phoenix and set up shop somewhere else. When I chose Milwaukee as my post-college location, it was mostly because one of my sisters lived there and then of course because it was someplace new.

And it gave me a good perspective, one that I could make it alone. It seems like I overcompensated for being so distant in age from my brother and sisters when I was growing up. Always the middle child. I think this affected me more drastically than I ever used to think. I guess I was lonely even in a crowd.

On the other hand, my reason for moving away from Phoenix and Matthews in the first place was because my life there had become too complex. There were too many friends and too many family members needing my attention. I was too popular, too in demand. I'm very serious. My boyfriend was a drunk, I hadn't gotten that disease yet at that point, and I was thought of by him as a "good person." What a condescending comment that had been from such an insincere person that it was almost funny. But that guy probably ended up dying of cirrhosis of the liver anyhow.

He had told me that he had actually loved his high school girlfriend the whole time he was dating me, even though she had moved to Alaska two years before. He told me upon dumping me that he was sure her child must have been his. I was humiliated, so I took a plane ride to Milwaukee and the snowy hills in that midwest town dominated by inclement weather.

But one thing I had forgotten was that you take yourself with you wherever you go. Kind of like that book <u>Wherever You Go, There You Are</u> by Jon Kabat Zinn, about Zen and being "mindful." How was I to know what downtown Milwaukee would be like? So bleak, and it was very dark, while the scent of beer from the breweries filled the air. And there were the trains going by all the time, with their whistles blowing in the night air. And I had no newspaper, telephone or TV.

It's a real mystery explaining my life there, especially why was I working at some hospital for those nine months? But I did buy a stereo. A good sign. And I "cooked" and read a lot. Much caulifower with condensed cheddar cheese soup for topping, little cans of meatballs to mix with Ragu spaghetti sauce. It may sound bad, but it was delicious to me at the time.

In fact, it was not long after my boyfriend broke up with me that I packed up and moved in with my oldest sister and her husband and daughter at that location, almost without thinking about it, certainly without an invitation. And it was after I had told them about all sorts of personal problems headed up by dropping out of Matthews where Ellen had gone to school.

And these were two very busy professionals. So of course there was no red carpet layed out for me once I got there, and I quickly wore out my welcome. And luckily I hadn't started drinking alcohol regularly at that time. God knows what might have happened if I had been into that.

Milwaukee might have been nice if you had a lot of money. I sensed that as time went by during those months living there. The stuff at the Boston Store and Gimbels looked enticing. In fact the former is where I got my Magnavox stereo. But when my sister and brother-in-law let me go, I had moved to a little run-down hotel at first in downtown Milwaukee called the Berlin Arms, not far from the hospital where I worked as a ward secretary. My brother-in-law had driven me to a bus stop to go out from there to find a job. It was a little off-kilter—but definitely understandable. And I experienced wonderful, hopeful feelings about children from knowing their little girl. She was so smart, and loved a "Big Bird" doll from the "Sesame Street" television show that I bought her.

But there I was, standing and freezing in my non-lined, corduroy coat, looking for somewhere to work. The bus had dropped me off in front of Children's Hospital, but they had no real openings. So I went across the street to Deaconess Hospital where I got a job right across the field from my future apartment that I sometimes think might have belonged later to Jeffrey Dahmer. I think he was on the second floor of an apartment right in that area. What a thought!

But Milwaukee was liveable for the most part. Of course now in 2000 you couldn't walk from Deaconess Hospital to downtown Milwaukee at night, maybe not even during the day. But there's always plenty to talk about with that stay, and I always like to point out that my job as a ward secretary at Deaconess was actually kind of fun, with some scary emergencies thrown in. And I got to read the <u>Tolkien Trilogy/Hobbit</u>.

In addition, Elton John came out with his "Honkey Chateau" album, with: "Rocket Man, burning out his fuse up here alone." Add to that whole picture that the winter of 1971-72 was one of Wisconsin's coldest winters on record, and it makes you wonder why I stayed there so long.

But being alone wasn't so bad. I think I learned to enjoy talking with people more because of that experience. People who know me best know I love to talk. Not in a savvy way like kidding waiters at restaurants, but a "How do you feel or think about that?" kind of conversation.

So the whole Milwaukee experience comes out as a positive thing in my life. And today, except for the "Get a job" mantra, I've actually never been happier in the 20 years since then. It's not worth worrying about things in the past, which as I've said is my absolutely worst habit.

CHAPTER 9

THE SIX YEAR BUILD-UP

The length of time between my lonely days in Milwaukee to moving back to Phoenix and marrying my husband was only two years. One irony was that Todd had actually grown up in Milwaukee, albeit in a more prosperous part of town; but that shared experience of living there drew us together when we were beginning to date.

Moving next door to him in an apartment close to Matthews University, he drove a bike as a student and I worked in Mesa and drove around in an old car. Part of why we ended up together is possibly because we were the same age, the same temperament, and had shared some of the same events in history. Members of the high school class of 1970 met up with me many times in my life since those pre-college days. But basically, I moved with two roommates to the apartment across the sidewalk from his. The rest is history, and Todd and I started our married life with a self- determined move to Washington, D.C.

The job that I started at the D.C. paper factory in July 1974 was interesting because I got to talk to lots of people and manage their accounts. I moved up the ladder there in a short time due to my accuracy when typing, and accuracy was especially important in those days before the personal computer. It's almost hard to believe that businesses in 1974 got along without what we now know as "word processing." What a boon that was.

But more intriguing than that was the strike against the factory in 1975 that for me went on longer than my employment there. And it was very significant that my heavy drinking began with that strike. Cases of beer started pouring into the clerical strike headquarters almost within the day of the start of the picket line.

That the strike was a year and a half of my life was also a bit unfathomable. I had led a pretty much conservative life up to that point. And I felt very strange when I later heard some of the higher up employees talking about how the packagers were "beneath" us clerical people. There had been some violence between the packagers and their supervisors after the midnight deadline in fall 1975. But I found out later that the paper company had been taunting the packagers, saying they were training strikebreakers to come in and do their jobs.

The first thing I noticed that early October morning, after the packager union had gone on strike at midnight the night before, was all of the distant noise from the crowds. There were TV crews there, drawn by the message that the packagers had destroyed some of the machinery upon leaving the building that morning. Also, some of the men had gotten into a fight with their supervisors.

A meeting was called for the clerical guild employees to vote if we were going to cross the picket line and go into work. That they called a meeting was the surprising part. Because as soon as the meeting started, the talk suddenly became "blue collar" and "white collar" employees; how we were not the former and should not condone violence. It must have been enough for the majority of the clerical people, as three-fourths of them went back in the building, walking right across the picket lines in the process.

I had often heard about "scabs" crossing picket lines, an opinion I shared almost out of faith. Unions are good—management is bad. But I didn't know. Certainly I was not going to go into work that day, after the confusing set of circumstances surrounding strikebreakers and violence and blue and white "collars." I just happened to run into the left-wing people, which I've always thought was fortunate for me.

I never thought much about the fact that the packagers may have wiped out the possibility of a successful strike due to the violence. For that first day the company had so much damage done to the machinery that it could no longer print paper to meet its orders. The company president would never forgive the packagers after that. Of course I didn't know that until late in the game.

During all of the partying some of us almost forgot we were talking about men's (and they were almost all white males) livelihoods. One of those packagers ended up despondent enough to kill himself. I went to the wake; I had hardly known him, but it was something I'll always remember. I then thought about the few times he had come to strike headquarters and I wonder how condemned he must have felt about the paper factory's blanket blacklisting of the packagers and him being only one year from retirement. And all of us partying.

One very fine aspect of the strike was that I got to meet a lifelong friend who headed up the clerical guild and was in charge of the clerical strike headquarters. She was also named Anne, so I became "Anne B" while she was "Anne G". A very outgoing and funny woman. She used to smoke cigarettes with a holder and keep things compelling and structured a bit in an otherwise open door of the strike office. She was a Gemini if that counts for anything, quicksilver and very well-spoken. She would often bring her two cildren in, and they managed to have a good time.

In the meantime, I was meeting and talking to union stewards and officers who also seemed very progressive. I had always thought of myself that way too, and felt some camaraderie there as well. I was relieved that other people besides my and Todd's friends were "cool" in the big city of Washington, D.C. Nobody would have guessed that in five or six years I would be in the throes of a frightening mental disease in that same city. For the time being, I was fitting in like I never had before.

One telling aspect of my abuse of alcohol was that it coincided with my sometimes indifferent attitude towards my husband. Early into the strike at strike headquarters I was reminded that I should pick Todd up at the airport like I said I would. Instead I practically yelled "Let him find another way home!"

Later "Anne G," the person heading up that whole effort for the clerical people, said she was very impressed by that, which didn't make sense to me really. But I appreciated the sentiment. She might have thought that I was simply being liberated or independent. Actually, I was selfishly having too good a time to pull myself away.

I must have also complained about my marriage to the packagers and other union people. One of whom some people called "blue collar workers" was friendly enough with me to tell me that some of the packagers were saying I was "fair game." Then he told me to go ahead and divorce Todd and go back to finish up my degree. Presumably, I was pro-union and Todd wasn't. That appeared to be the gist of his reasoning.

Actually, through all of that, Todd was doing the financing and for his part, was mostly supportive for my new venture. He had only known me as a hard worker at the jobs I had held since knowing him. There was the ward clerk at St. John's Hospital, the postal clerk at the post office and the clerical job at the paper factory. In his mind he just worried about my lost salary.

So, partly to ease Todd's queasiness, I got a part-time job as a secretary with a chemical workers union. There were probably those who were more deserving, but the people who worked there loved me and everything about me. They thought I should try to be a union organizer once I got divorced. There was that constant and underlying thread of my unhappiness in my marriage. They said I had the personality and mind set that would inspire workers to sign up to be "union" wherever I went. With that pressure, though, I would probably have "snapped" much sooner. Then again, though I couldn't have handled it anyway, being a union organizer would probably have been no more intense than my future race into a continuous psychotic break at college.

My job with those men from the chemical union was fun; they even let me pick my own salary which I said should be $5 per hour, a good wage back in 1975. There was also an interesting perk: getting to go with two of the bosses to a <u>Rolling Stone Magazine</u>'s Christmas party. There was plenty to eat and drink and the next morning I appeared on the front page of the morning newspaper's "social pages." It was a good portrayal, with me holding a gin and tonic in my hand and talking to two men. I had become a stereotype of myself.

One thing that had become obvious that I wanted to be like my friend, Anne G., busy with union business. At one point during a convention it came down to our minor little group of four or five women getting a powerful negotiator to step down from his job and admit his mistakes during the strike. When it was his turn to speak at the conference, he announced that he would be quitting his job. Looking back, I don't even remember what it was that he was supposed to have done wrong, except for making members of the union sign charges against those specific workers inside the factory who had crossed the picket line. In any case, I now had an enemy in that negotiator.

In the end, the strike was a very tempestuous time for everybody involved. I made some odd friends, fleeting as several of them turned out to be. But it was a high energy vocation being somebody "on strike," and maybe part of my becoming a schizophrenic years later. Again I was standing on the outside, just how I did with my family throughout my entire life. So there was a six year build-up from the beginning of the strike and my drunkeness to my first being committed to a mental hospital.

One thing I learned was that my foremost thoughts should have been more with my own husband, but I often was involved in "causes." It was as if in growing up in conservative Arizona I hadn't marched for peace or wore black armbands or went to political rallies enough. The only thing I remember before I became a left-winger with the strike was going on one march from downtown Phoenix to the Capitol Building protesting the Vietnam war in 1969 or 1970.

In another scene altogether, I was looking through my senior year annual (which I had to borrow since I had thrown everything away) and saw that there was practically no male students with long hair in our high school. I suppose that was true. And us girls wore uniforms and so forth, so it seems like a strike in downtown Washington, D.C. was an astonishing experience for me looking back before the days where I met Todd and moved east.

Towards the end of my "working" with the clerical union, they gave me a very silly, make-work task to keep me busy while they picked the brain of the saavy Nancy G. So I was kind of a joke looking back at that situation, writing and pinning addresses of people who had crossed the picket line on a big map of the Washington area. But it was still a very important time for me since it was important in leading up to my "nervous breakdown." Taking up binge drinking had been a fiasco, changing the entire tone of my life. Meeting all the fine people I did, however, was a very good thing.

CHAPTER 10

MOVING ON

I'm not sure when I actually realized it was time to start something new after all of the raucousness of being on strike for 18 months. I still felt I did the right thing, but it was almost only us two "Anne's" who were left of the clerical guild still out, and Anne G. had started looking too.

So back in those days I was good at finding new jobs, and I had two offers in my first day of interviewing. One was with a doctor's office and the other a national association. I took the first offer, the secretarial job where I didn't have to start until nine and where my boss, Daniel, ended up really appreciating me.

He as an alcoholic too, keeping a bottle of vodka in his desk to pull out and drink any time he wanted. So there was another kind of camaraderie there, a little like the strike, but just between the two of us. He said he didn't have to worry that I would strike, since there were no unions, and he hired me without consulting anyone. During the interview we both smoked a cigarette, a testament to how long ago 1976 was.

I was always in and out of jobs. But back in November 1976 or so, for the strike to end, and for me to become happy, active and successful again in a new work role was somewhat surprising. So I became a membership secretary.

It was a three person office, and Daniel's assistant, Brenda, had wanted to be the one to make the final choice in hiring. Whether she would have picked me is debatable, but there was immediate tension in the office with Brenda resenting me for having gotten Daniel to bypass her input. She might have resolved to get even somehow.

Almost immediately, I started hearing from her about my one year of college and lack of credentials. Brenda and Daniel both had degrees, Daniel a Ph.D. and Brenda a bachelor's. What did she want? She said I was considered "clerical support staff" even though there were only the three of us in that office. I did try to play that role for her, but it didn't come naturally. I had "too strong of a personality" for clerical work, as some supervisor later suggested.

My alcoholic streak was very strong during my days at the association. But it was a formal office, so I couldn't sit there and drink beer after beer like I had at strike headquarters. I had to be subtle about it, and often went to lunch with Todd and had a few. It was comforting for me to have a boss who was also an alcoholic. Once when they were returning from lunch they mentioned that my eyes seemed "glazed over."

Another big turning point at that job was the convention in New Orleans, to which Todd had decided not to go. I got a huge room overlooking the Mississippi River that had big tugboats moving about in the water. I was on an expense account, so that made the trip even more enjoyable. Daniel had come up with something that I could attend to while there, so I manned an office with information about the placement service that was available through our office in Washington, D.C. This was something I had handled in my job.

The booze was rampant at the convention in Daniel's room and at our headquarters. Since it was free and plentiful, I kept quite happy in spite of being alone there. There was a bar in the hotel with dancing, and I mostly hung out there, dancing with the various field counselors of the association. I drank so much one night that I didn't get up in time the next morning for Daniel's big speech. But he said that was OK. Looking back, that wasn't very nice of me.

All the while, Brenda would introduce me as "Daniel's and my secretary." Thinking back on that woman, I remember somebody taking pictures in our office, and she wanted at least two of her leaning over my shoulders to see what I was doing. I used to complain a lot about Brenda to Todd and our friends, but it really was true that the woman was a pompous ass, so worked up about herself and the other "professionals." That word and Brenda's obsession with it had finally become so trite. However, I was pretty upbeat at the convention, because I was surrounded by others who didn't care about whether I was support staff or not.

There was one very good, tourist type of day and night when I went with Daniel and his friends to Bourbon Street, aptly named. Drinks in hand, they said they wanted to see what kind of jazz I liked. There was lots of dancing and drunkenness, and when we got back to the hotel, I naively went up with one of the field counselors to his room.

I was dumb enough to actually dance with him. Then I stopped to think, I realized that I shouldn't be there. I just said, "You've got to meet my husband, Todd. He's a really nice guy." I repeated this twice before he let me go. I hurried to the door with an "I'll see you tomorrow"—and I should have known better.

All in all, it was a good trip, though I spent more time at the hotel than I should have. The bar up on the top of the hotel had a band that pretended to be a Las Vegas act. It was OK with me, since they played some familiar tunes, but I probably could have spent my time better walking around downtown New Orleans. On my last day there I finally did.

I made it obvious to others that I was an alcoholic while at that conference just as I had done at a party at Daniel's house a few months earlier. I danced and got drunk with whoever was around at the hotel bar, though I did make it to a dinner once with the group at one of the restaurants converted from an old house. We were eating beef, and Brenda and her husband ordered white wine while I ordered red. Daniel and his friends repeated what they had said about me having class. They really wanted to like me, it seemed. And I guess they did.

On the plane back to D.C., I sat with the student assistant who was in the association's office for the summer. We had a talk about our husbands, hers was an "ex." I told her that Todd and I were "just buddies;" the student said she divorced her husband because he didn't spend enough time with her. Almost opposite problems. The woman seemed embarrassed when the plane arrived at Dulles Airport and Todd was there to give us a ride home. He looked strange to me until I realized that he had just gotten a haircut.

***

While I worked for the association, Todd and I had some great friends. It had been good living in Washington, D.C. There was James, in the same apartment complex with the keg to finish off on Sunday mornings. He was a very good guitar player with a strong voice and was one of the funniest of people. It was good to know somebody with the same interests and inclinations. We went to bars often, drinking beer and listening to other singers with guitars. That was an important past time, with the three of us loving music so much.

Then there was Karl the hippy, a title he didn't mind. He had just moved to the area and was an officemate of Todd's. He quickly became one of our best friends. Very left wing, he supported the Sandanistas and hated the injustices towards all sorts of people. He's somebody who actually thinks Native Americans were the rightful owners of the country. He's a good guy.

We played volleyball every week with the group of acquaintances/friends from the best of the upper-middle class and us everyday revelers. Of course "Anne G" and her family also remained the best of friends even after the strike. There was also Molly and Skip with the golden retriever, who were the first people we met when moving from Phoenix to D.C. Those friends and more shared the "20 something" days of our lives which were special to many of us, even in retrospect.

During 1976 and 1977, the very intense years of these friendships, Todd was in a job he didn't like at all. That in itself could have been very bad, but during those days he had a knack for taking his job less seriously. He started late and took at least an hour for lunch, though he claimed only 30 minutes. This was something that stayed consistent during his career—nobody seemed to mind. There was so much activity in our lives that we worked all day and played through the night.

I was also in a work situation I didn't like. The "professional/support staff" nonsense continued the whole year and a half that I was with the association. Daniel seemed to look the other way when it came to that. For example, at one of my performance reviews Daniel offered me a $1,000 raise, which was later vetoed by Brenda. I started to realize that I ought to go back and get a degree if it was something that bothered me. And it did. I knew that I was as smart and professional as my blowhard, insecure co-worker. Besides, getting a degree was something people seemed to expect from me. All of that sounds very shallow of me, I realize. Why did I give a damn what she thought?

In March of 1978, though we wouldn't be leaving D.C. to go to Arizona until May, Todd and I decided to quit our jobs. That gave us a few months to party before leaving all of our friends behind. Matthews University in Phoenix was where I would finish getting my degree, or so I thought. The two of us threw a huge going away party in May and the next morning breakfasted with James in a diner before leaving. By then, I had been an alcoholic for about three years and was definitely enjoying myself.

Upon leaving, Todd and I drove to Wisconsin where his parents and sisters lived. We stayed for almost a month in the boat house right off the lake near his parents' home. It was very nice of them to put us up. One high point was when Todd and I went to see Bob Marley in concert. For some reason I was concerned with what we were going to wear, and thought that it would be completely overcrowded and wild there. But I was wrong and we had a great time seeing the Rastafi singer. Being worried was already starting to put too much pressure on me—and for no reason, that's the strange part. I had a pretty perfect life. The morning Todd and I prepared to leave for Phoenix, around June 1978, Todd's mother confronted me and told me that I had no sense of humor and was always negative. The criticism went on for about a half hour. I had said, "Well, how about your other son John? He always has a negative attitude." She simply replied, "But he's just being funny."

In any case, I made myself cry while Todd was down at the boat house. I know you can never say that somebody "made me cry." His father and sister, Paulette, also listened in—everybody but Todd. I decided wisely not to put up much of an argument. What can one say? But we left with me crying my eyes out as we were giving our goodbyes.

Leaving all that behind we were happily on our way to our new destination, a somewhat brave move. Neither of us had any prospect for a job and had only our savings to live on. Live on it we did. We bought a beautiful townhouse in Phoenix, our second choice after losing out on the "Pebble Beach" house we were too late to buy and would always remember. But in our lives, things would have been so different if we had made a couple of real estate moves.

But the Los Molinos place was a two story home with a balcony encircling the living area. People were impressed. We just loved it. And I was thrilled about our beautiful and tiny back yard. For the only time ever in my life I liked doing the yard work.

On the other hand, I was getting ready for the big push at college—planning to finish my degree as rapidly as possible and majoring in something marketable. So Todd and I thought, why not a "marketing major?" (How silly.) I got accepted to and pre-registered at Matthews University for the fall semester of 1978 with that specific major in mind if you can believe that. I knew what I needed to sign up for my first semester at the college of business. One of the courses required for all business majors was economics, and Todd had recommended that one teacher, Dr. Lawrence Brown. He had given him a B in his economics course back when Todd was at Matthews in 1974. I signed up for that course with that teacher, which turned out to be a very significant move for me.

It really didn't take long for me to start showing an obsessive kind of behavior toward professors of economics. I would sit in that big class of Professor Brown's and think that he was "inspiring." I later sent him a letter from D.C. that told him so. Even though Brown was Todd's friend, every time he asked me about Todd's job search, I took it as an interest in me. In fact, once when he asked how Todd was doing, I gave him a dejected look. He then asked about me or so I thought. It was an attitude of mine that followed me around the campus. I thought I was smart and seemed to want to prove it to everybody, especially Dr. Brown.

The oddest aspect of my attitude was how Todd lived with that kind of behavior. He probably at times thought that he wasn't very important in my life and I know he was aware of my "crushes" on those two professors by my last year of college. But he was kind about it with a "What is Anne up to now?" type of affectionate concern. Those were days when Todd was very loving towards me.

Back at Matthews University, following the tearful goodbye to Todd's family, things went well. It hadn't gotten to the post-nervous breakdown days as far as Todd's attitude toward me, so we were both siting pretty in Phoenix in "School Year 1978-79." I was taking a full 18-hour schedule, mostly Business College courses. Plus a fun course in English called Advanced Composition. That's about as close to a "creative writing" class that I ever took.

My weakness had always been quantitative courses like mathematics, though, and I dreaded the results of a test given to us students who weren't sure if we were prepared for specific levels of math. It came back that I was right on the border for pre-calculus versus "intermediate algebra," a much less difficult class. Concerned about grades, I decided to go with the algebra which I took and finished with an A.

That course would later come back to bother me, as Tydings in Washington, D.C. wasn't prepared to accept those hours as part of my transfer credits later in my last semester before graduation. I thank God for a letter I sent and got a return response from the chairman of the math department at Matthews. I guess Tydings didn't think it was "rigorous" enough to qualify for credit there. He set them straight.

There was already that running theme, that I began to overdo my college effort with a routine that was excessive. After classes, I re-wrote my notes and used four different highlighter colors for the different types of facts. For example, orange was for special and unusual tidbits of knowledge, or it was sometimes for "QFC" (questions from the class). The most specific details were always in yellow. Any time I'd bother reading the book, my highlighters kept me busy there as well. And it worked for me, that's the amazing part. Whether I really learned is very debatable. Of course I used to say I did.

I put myself through the wringer, and certain questions come to mind. For example, why the big hurry with the over challenging, 18-hour semesters? Todd had some high hopes for a decent income for me after college, so maybe that was it. But I didn't have to become such a people pleaser. There's just no point in being "the high A in the class"—which was one of my delusional goals.

In reality, I really wasn't that good a student. Class discussions, questions for the teacher or even reading the textbook for reference were weak areas for me. I just wrote down virtually everything that was said or put on the blackboard by the teacher. I knew I didn't have much time, so I wrote everything down so I could go back later and re-learn every fact. And there was very little that would be on the tests and quizzes that wasn't presented in class. Later, in 1981, however, I threw all of those notes out. Probably the worst thing about the purge.

So, while I sought nirvana at Matthews, Todd looked for a job. It was good that we had saved enough money to tide us through a whole year. Rather than money, though, I was more concerned that Professor Brown let me and the other students see his tests from the same class one year earlier. He said they had been distributed to some students illegally the previous year and he just wanted to make things fair. It was true, they made great study guides.

Alcohol and college were a strange mix that first return to college semester at Matthews University. Beer was still my drink of choice when studying, though it was not yet time for the all night study marathons with beer and wine. That would come later. As it was, I looked drawn for school every day due to my drinking, a dead giveaway to anybody who bothered to notice. Talk about "glazed" looks.

Todd and I developed a daily routine. He would drive me to school, drop me off by the business building and then take off to search for a job. I would go to my classes and get out in time to go to the student union cafeteria before heading to class again. There I would always have Mexican food with lots of hot sauce. And I would study—even while eating lunch. I was actually having a great time, feeling that the effort was well worth it. And you know, I don't think I was certifiably mentally ill yet.

I had certain obsessive behaviors, but there were definitely no solid delusions yet. I guess except for the fact I always thought everyone was in love with me. I seemed to have that as a problem. In fact, maybe my older sister was right about me when I was in eighth grade. I did think I was Gina Lollabridga or some other kind of siren. In my high school photo I had all my hair brushed forward and a slight sideways tilt of my head. Even my 18-year-old son Phillip thought I looked rather vain. Certainly no type of Claudia Schiffer thing going on, so don't ask me why. I must have been cut out to think big and keep losing out in the getting along with people thing.

I was really naive in the way I approached getting a college degree. I was a quiet person, and never would have challenged anything the teachers said because I was too reticent. I was also too self-conscious about standing out because I was 26 years old, as old as many of the assistant professors. But on the whole, I felt fairly anonymous in college, which was how I liked it. And as far as my having crushes on a few of the teachers at my age, that was obviously embarrassing. But like I said, I had not become psychotic yet.

There wasn't much happening with my family that fall semester of 1978. There were occasional dinners on Sunday at my parents' house, but that was about it. Todd and I were enjoying life although he wasn't finding a job. He even looked up old friends as part of the effort, and the best man from our wedding offered him some clerical job paying $9,000 per year. During that semester, we got a visit from our best friend, James, along with a friend of all of us. They had a pretty good time though they didn't get to see that much of me, since I was being intense about school already.

At one point that year, Todd's parents offered to buy the house from us and charge us rent for living there, but I nixed that idea as something that would give Todd's parents too much control. It also probably wouldn't have worked out all that well anyhow with the way Todd's mother had felt about me the previous summer.

During that sophomore year of my Bachelor's degree, there was no evidence of a future mental breakdown except for my crush on Professor Brown. Even that was only barely perceptible to others. It foreshadowed the same kind of trap I would fall into at Tydings a year later, when I was obsessed with not only school, but with "academia"—and Malcom Collins of course. I should have been more savvy.

All the while that Todd and I were living on the $10,000 we had saved, our money was pouring out on things like textbooks, out-of-state tuition, mortgage payments, restaurants, liquor and music. We were living high and both deserved it in return for being in the work force for so long, especially Todd. He really tried to get a job, but it just didn't work out.

As a payback for all the studying that first semester, I got six A's. I was proud. Todd and I went into Professor Brown's office to tell him the good news. He didn't really know what to say—I had been obsessed with grades in his class too. But he just said that it was a hard thing to do. I will never forget that Todd said, "She had a little help," meaning him, and I had snapped back at him. Dr. Brown had looked embarrassed. What did I want, an award?

So by the end of 1978, I had been back to college for one semester. My extremism in life had found one more method of transmission—through my being a student. Did I belong there? Maybe not. But at least I was doing something productive in spite of my very eccentric nature.

I had noticed certain things that had changed from the time when I dropped out in fall 1971 to how things were in fall 1978. For one thing, my freshman dormitory had been turned into an office building. But more importantly, looking around I noticed how beautiful the campus was. I had never really paid that much attention before. And of course I was about seven years older than other students in my classes. I'm still not sure whether or not that was an advantage. Probably not. I had added world experience, but I had also gotten "rusty" as far as being accountable as a student to have memorized some basic facts.

But it all worked well for me. I was having a grand old time. And that poor economics professor I was practically "stalking" was probably glad that I moved back to D.C when I did one full semester later. Time enough before, though, to take the second introduction to economics course from him.

A funny thing was that I actually spoke to him on the phone from work one day in 1986, eight years later. He said he was using my editorial from where I worked in one of his economics classes. To be honest, I didn't want to talk about it, but he said the people where I worked would miss me when I left, that I had done a real good job. I said something about the article having been "rather un-academic," and he chuckled.

Then I finished by saying, "As usual, we'll send you a Christmas card with a picture of Phillip." (Which we did for a few years for some reason.) He said, "I'll look forward to that." That's the last time I would ever take up any more of that man's time.

CHAPTER 11

ENTERING THE FRAY

In spring 1979 at Matthews University I felt that my life was going to be important and that I should be able to perform at a high level academically for whatever might happen next. That sounds melodramatic—lots of students feel that way. But I was sure that I would be singled out. I wasn't frantic about it yet, though, and I wasn't that "crazy" either; but the idea was still there. Everything was about <u>me</u>.

Fall semester 1978 had been hard, and I had gotten all A's, so I suppose I was starting to feel untouchable, that I could handle anything anyone wanted to throw my way. But as I've said, who knows what I had really learned, partly because I was drinking a little more every week.

By spring 1979 I certainly felt that I fit in there with Matthews and academia. I was not intimidated at all by the various professors, and I had already started an eeiry build-up of self-important thoughts. Was there some chance that I was growing into schizophrenia all of my life?

One of my six sisters likes to tell people how "weird" I was when we were all growing up. There was a metal, yellow chair in our backyard. I used to use a big belt and strapped my sisters in the chair and then I would rotate the chair around and around talking about the sun and the "nine planets." I would name and say something about each one. Pretty strange, I must admit, but maybe it was also an innocent fascination with astronomy. But it's something my brother and sisters laugh about today.

I feel a little wistful now when my younger sisters talk about their chidhoods and what funny things the four of them did. And my parents have a picture of the oldest three children, a beautiful portrait that was recast as the classy shot that it was. I don't think I can say enough about that.

I definitely love my family, I just regret being almost a forced loner. That's what they always say about the murderer or other kinds of criminals. They ask the neighbors or even the family, and the response is always, "He or she was a 'loner,' always kept to himself."

For Todd, it had been a discouraging time as far as the job hunt went in school year 1978-79. Being a former federal worker was no help at all. In D.C. he had his pick of jobs, but in Phoenix there just weren't that many opportunities. He did get into Century 21 as a real estate agent, and he sold a few homes.

When I look back, I hope it was at least a little bit fun for him too, being somewhere like Phoenix with the nice weather, my family, the beautiful townhouse, and so on. Truth is I probably didn't concentrate much on that. It no doubt was a negative experience for Todd since the very next summer after moving to Phoenix we had to return to Washington, D.C. because he couldn't find a job. It was kind of embarrassing to have to turn back and undo such a big move. But he held his head high as he should have.

Spring semester 1979 was no exception to the phenomenon of me being grandiose about grades. I picked out six courses that would help me get a marketing degree from the college of business. They were a challenging line-up; things not required were undertaken by me for show or for when I would move on to "graduate school."

I had so big an ego that I would sometimes point out to the teachers the way the material presented in the classroom should be tested. Mostly that it should be the <u>only</u> material on the test. I went to that marketing professor's office after getting my B at the end of spring 1979 and told him that because of his lack of follow-up of his lectures with tests, I got the only B out of my 12 classes that school year. He said, "It happens to the best of us." Period. In real life I suppose it didn't need to be a big deal, even to me.

But in Spring semester 1979, I was going around school with a bounce in my step. I still had a crush on Professor Brown, teacher of my "econ" courses. One thing that had changed when I went into my second class with him was that I no longer sat towards the back of the class. I had moved up to the second row, and it was a much smaller classroom. I felt in part that my sitting there probably made him feel a little nervous, and that he simply didn't let it show.

That second economics class was just like the first, in that I never discussed anything or asked questions. I was much too quiet and busy getting everything down in writing. As I've said, I thought that at the end of the whole college period of my life I could actually self-teach myself, all because right then I had to be in a hurry for some now unclear reason.

My studying for tests and taking notes were activities during which I can now say I was "manic." In 1982, Dr. Crow, the every-Saturday psychiatrist, tried to get me to believe that I had specifically acted that way. The whole "Lithium" theory. I never pinpointed any days like that for him, though he clearly wanted me to, but the college obsession had just become a way of life for me. I had always thought I was just being an "enthusiastic student."

So in summer 1979 Todd had done what he had to do—go back to work for his old employer. It had been pretty easy for him to secure a job there. We packed up everything and sent it on its way back east via a moving van. No sooner had that happened that the man who would be Todd's new boss called to tell him that he had changed his mind and didn't want to hire him after all. It was unbelievable. The only thing Todd could say was "Too bad!" It was unfortunate that his employer had to start off their relationship like that. Of course he had to let Todd come on board again, and Todd and I wrapped things up in Phoenix.

One of the things that I wanted to take care of was to tell Professor Brown that Todd and I would be leaving Phoenix. The spring semester was over and that meant another trip to his office. I had also put on my spaghetti strap sun dress to tell him that we were leaving town. I had always thought I was so "sexy." I told him, "I was going to ask you to be my advisor if we had been sticking around." This was after telling him that economics is the only major in the business college that's at all "humanitarian." He had agreed and we laughed about my initial decision to major in marketing.

"Well, I would have been glad to be your advisor if you had been errr…'sticking around'." Then the big moment for me came when I reached out to shake his hand. At that moment I looked up and saw Professor Brown's partner giving me an icy stare. As I walked away Brown said to me, "Let me know how everything turns out." Another bad foreboding.

The night before we left Phoenix to move back to Washington, D.C., there was a fire across the street from our house. I screamed at Todd, trying to be heard. I saw a big group of people watching the fire and watching me. I got very worked up over the scene in front of our house. After the fires were out, Todd and I lingered on the back porch of our little yard. The next morning we would be leaving. We had no choice because the new family was moving in that day.

I was depressed because we had to move. I was really attached to that house because we had been able to hang onto it without anybody's help. And the place had appreciated so much that we had to borrow hardly any money from Todd's parents. But we did borrow some, and that too came back to haunt us. We needed money for the brittle little townhouse in Silver Spring, Maryland. We later lost so much money on that place it was pitiful, though that misfortune didn't seem to matter to anyone but Todd and me. Our misfortune was uniquely ours.

Those few months following the spring semester of 1979 were the only break from college courses and all the studying that I would have until after graduating three semesters later. I got to take off that summer, with Todd and me driving back east not knowing what the atmosphere would be at work or which college I would attend once we arrived.

Consequently, our attempt to move to Arizona was a failure in a certain sense, though maybe it was a good thing for Todd and me to get away from Matthews after just one year. Who knows what would have happened with the Professor Brown crush? Perhaps he wouldn't have been so "professional" as Professor Malcom Collins pretended to be a year later after realizing an older and doting undergraduate student was infatuated with him.

Once Professor Collins figured that one out about me in 1980, he more or less molded the situation to help him get tenure at Tydings. The only problem was that I didn't know about it. And I have to remember that to me things just "seemed" to be the case as I interpret it. How would anybody be able to prove it? However, I wouldn't bump into Collins until Valentine's Day 1980. I had enough trouble to deal with in 1979.

Todd and I drove into Washington, D.C. on July 5, 1979, and it was strange that there were fireworks going on at the mall, then we found out that the festivities had been rained out the day before. The first stop was at our old apartment building to see if James was home, and he wasn't.

So we rode into Washington, D.C. to see if Skip and Molly were at their apartment in the complex where we would rent a place until we were settled. They weren't home either. So we hung out at a small bar nearby, drinking beer and eating pizza.

I was feeling a winy sort of upset due to circumstances forcing a move back. We had left D.C. with the understanding that we would not be returning. However, when we finally got together with our friends and into our new apartment, we cheered up. It was a nice, small, and a furnished efficiency apartment in a very good part of town that they had found for us as a temporary place to stay.

It was good to see our friends again. They lived in the same complex a few buildings away. As always, living with them was

"DC" the golden retriever that they loved so much. And we would visit them on a farm in Indiana about three years later. That's how it was in the capitol, lots of moving around.

Within days of moving back, Todd and I would meet up with our left-wing good friend Karl and our other beer buddy James. The feelings were mixed. They enjoyed the reunion, but this time it was with the understanding that things just hadn't worked out. There had been a strange unraveling of events.

We had moved out of D.C. in May 1978 that first time at our peak of popularity. We threw a huge party a few days before leaving, and now we were back. Like James said much later during a 1998 visit to D.C., "Been there. Done that." He said that because Todd was considering moving back again then if he had gotten the job he was "temping" for. The day Philip found out that Todd did not get that job, he went over to our CD player and put on Beethoven's "Ode to Joy." He and I loved our lives in Phoenix, especially in 1998.

But back to summer 1979, I guess nobody likes a loser. Although we wanted either Karl, James or Anne G. over to our house every Saturday night like in the old days, it just didn't happen. Life had gone on for Todd and me too, but here we were now trying to fit right back in where we had left off. Just too much had transpired for everyone. There were at least a few awkward silences. Sure they were still our friends. It was just different—what would one expect?

Another big question on my mind that summer of 1979, was what to do about continuing with my degree. At first I thought that I would be going to a private college in the fall 1979 semester. In pursuit of that, I called the friend of Professor Brown at that college and set up an appointment. When I got there he said Prof. Brown had told him that I was a "good student." He then called the director of admissions to be in on the evaluation of my courses taken at Matthews. Things were very proper. In reality, it's probably the professors who least like the school girl crush. Most teachers that is.

From the very beginning of the transcript analysis, the professors seemed to have made up their minds to discourage me from transferring there. They ridiculed the names of some of my courses: With Theory of Arithmetic, they said, "If they had just called it something else." With Environmental Horticulture, "Isn't all horticulture environmental?" And of course they wouldn't accept Intermediate Algebra, which was self-taught, or my astronomy course where I had gotten a "D." In all, the two professors there were going to deny me credit for 12 semester hours, and I would have had no possibility of graduating in December 1980 like Todd and I had planned. That changed everything.

For one thing, I would have been in no state of mind after the fall semester 1980 to graduate from any college. Of course I didn't know that a year and a half earlier. But I had planned to graduate in December 1980 and had no inclination to change those plans because of two snooty professors.

I decided to meet with someone from the economics department at Tydings University in Washington, D.C. His name was Professor Kelton and he said that a private school is usually better than a public university, but in my case that did not apply. The economics program at Tydings was highly ranked nationally.

And while he was telling me how impressive Tydings was, I was telling him how impressive I was. I pointed out that getting 11 out of 12 A's during those last two semesters at Matthews, which was a very "rigorous" school, was quite an accomplishment. I probably sounded ridiculous.

Professor Kelton called me a "hot shot." I showed him my list of courses for the next semester, and he thought I was being way too easy on myself if I was aiming to graduate in three semesters plus two summer sessions. He had me move into calculus right away and signed me up for four economics courses that fall semester 1979, including both "macro" and "micro" intermediate "core" courses in that one semester. What was he trying to prove? In any case, I decided to go ahead and try for the challenge, even though it was clear that he was sticking me with as hard a line-up as he could. It certainly seemed that way to me.

I tried to understand the whole, overall picture of all economic theory at one time. What a bind to be in though. But at the same time I was trying to "consume large quantities" of economics, my grades that semester included a B and C, definitely not what I had planned. I seemed shocked to learn that I was at another "difficult" university. I was not really prepared for that fall 1979 semester there, even though I gave it my all.

Tydings had a huge and beautiful campus, and I walked briskly on weekdays across the campus. It was a long walk, but I always made it to class on time. How I ended up cheerfully working towards a degree at the close of my three semesters in the shape I was in was an intriguing question. I wasn't an ordinary student, but one who was obsessed with math, statistics and economic theory. But still I had just that one semester of relative normalcy left to revel in. My future seemed bright to me, as I've said, because I was so sure that I would be "important" because of my efforts.

I was able to talk to the teachers at that school, seemingly unimpressed by them, but I wanted to impress somebody, the more prestigious the credentials of the teacher, the better. Professor Kelton was a graduate of Harvard, Professor Welding was from Berkeley, etc. Could it have been Brenda and her "clerical support staff" obsession at the association that drove me to become such an intense and pompous student? Maybe that was a part of it. I always sought approval. Where that came from, I don't know, because I had had a fairly successful life.

One significant point is that I had no "crushes" on any of the Tydings professors during my first semester there. I was still trying to accomplish something that would impress Dr. Brown back in Phoenix, under the impression that he was one of the smartest teachers from either school.

It's funny that I had picked Todd's major as my own. He got his B.S. degree in economics in 1974 from Matthews just a week before we got married and moved to Washington. But when we got married, I was a college drop-out. And I had only met Todd's parents a few days before. Not a good Lutheran girl, but I would have to do. But with our shared major, I was most challenged by the math and statistics. For one thing, I wasn't very good at either of those two subjects.

The whole time I was making an ass of myself at Tydings, I was still drinking heavily. I remained on that alcoholic roller coaster that began back with the strike at the paper factory. School and booze had become my thing and I tried to combine them subtley. I drank beer while re-writing my notes after class each day, up until bedtime, which usually came late. I got in a better mood as I drank more beer.

I also ran in place to music for a break from studying. Music, booze, studying—I never got sleepy, and made it all part of the routine. That kind of behavior wasn't unique to Tydings, because I had behaved the same way at Matthews. Mine were highly- "medicated" grades.

While I was drinking up university life, I developed some strange leanings for such a scholarly student. I liked astrology back then, read mine and Todd's and our friends' horoscopes in the paper each day. I knew which signs were in my planets, like Venus in Taurus or Jupiter in Scorpio, etc. I also watched two hour-long soap operas each day and planned my schedule around them. I think they were "Days of Our Lives" and "As the World Turns." So much for the "impressive" student being that thoughtful in all corners of her life. Again, looking back, I seemed a bit dense. If I ever catch a glimpse of a soap opera since then, I've always thought they seemed pretty dumb.

But I was taking in the whole college experience at Tydings, including the weather. When there was snow on the ground and ice on the sidewalks, I was careful not to fall like I had in past winters on a few occasions. I kept warm with a rust colored down jacket that was like a uniform for me; I wore it every day. And I was also vain. I bought a book bag that was teal blue with black piping, then realized later that the jacket and book bag didn't match at all. I was upset about not matching, I even went to the store with my parka and tried to trade it for a blue one. So on top of everything else, I looked silly.

Another embarrassing thing for me was that my stomach started to growl loudly during class time. Everybody could hear it. So I started eating antacid tablets in between classes, though the noise still got a lot worse as time went on. So much for Tums.

Teachers at Tydings started to notice me as far back as the fall semester 1979, though it could have been nothing more than just wondering what all the noise was about. They also saw me taking profuse notes and taking so many economics courses, and could probably tell that I was a 27-year-old woman rather than the standard college junior of 21 years old.

Professor Welding, one older economics teacher, took an interest in my love of the subject he was teaching. A few times I would see the scrutiny and think it gave me privileges beyond the every day students. For example, once I called Professor Welding at his home the night before a test, and he didn't seem to know what to say.

Some other teachers were noticing me too, or at least I thought so, but not from my enthusiasm. Once again, my face would clearly show (to those who noticed) that I was hung over from drinking the night before. That happened often. The look on my face depended on when I went to bed the night before. But in spite of the constant drinking, I stayed successful with grades in school, keeping up the pace begun a year earlier at Matthews, using my same methods.

All in all, I found myself in a very high profile atmosphere at Tydings that fall 1979 semester. Not only had I transferred mid-stream from another college, I had gone home and back again across the country. My life was as complex as anyone's I knew.

Never a very easygoing student since returning to college, now was no different. As an example of my attitude about Tydings, I spent all my research time in the graduate library, figuring I would find a better, more academic atmosphere there than at the undergraduate library. It could also have been that there were older students there and I felt more comfortable. But looking back, it might be that I thought I was as remarkable as any graduate student—that same old thing.

Amidst the college scene, Todd and I decided to go house hunting, hoping to find a deal like we had in Phoenix. We had certainly loved that place. We were supposed to move out of the efficiency apartment once a place was found. We went to a place in the suburbs of Maryland and found an interesting townhouse for sale.

It needed work, but we liked it right away, with nice carpeting, two stories and all. We had believed that we would never find a good deal in the D.C. area, and now thought we had. Todd and I even waited there with the wife for her husband to come home and talk about our "offer." We wanted to snap up the place.

While we definitely had second thoughts before we bought since we had to rent for a month, the place seemed all right for the time being. We had added all sorts of extras, like refinishing the floors. There was a few good things about it. It had two bedrooms, one of which I turned into my study room and where I would spend much of my time. And there were oak parquet floors. But that was about it on the positive side.

The bathroom was upstairs and the walls between the houses were only as thick as between bedrooms in a normal house. In the morning, I could hear both Todd and the man next door clearing their throats and brushing their teeth. It was annoying. Once we had the radio on in the bathroom and the man next door called to say he could hear it loud and clear.

The fact that Todd lived there too made it bearable. I might have been able to talk a good game out of my nonchalance about him, flirting with all kinds of men, but in reality, he was the one person I loved more than anyone. Why I never wanted to let him know that back then was a big mystery. We could definitely have used more "gentle" moments together during that time when I was a student at Tydings.

Todd was working a full-time job and I was stressing out over school. We both worked hard, but I had a whole lot more fun, at least I think so. I have some pictures of me at that time, and I hadn't yet actually begun the downward spiral. That definitely started up on "V-Day," for happy valentine that next spring semester 1980. How bizzare. I seemed destined to get myself in over my head.

Fall semester of 1979 ended successfully in a way. Todd and I still had our mental and physical health and we still had each other. Little did we know that we would need a lot of strength to confront the kind of year 1980 would become. In retrospect, I would look back and envy my relative state of rest and sanity before then.

That whole aspect of worrying myself to death, analyzing situations, wondering if I was doing the right thing—that started <u>way</u> before 1980. And maybe I had been "kind and good," but most people know those traits don't get you much of anything. And of course there was my family loneliness.

But 1980 was on its way in, and that's when my "weirdness" became something more. In the truest sense, I guess it was "fate" for me to become a schizophrenic. That's probably the most simple way to explain it.

CHAPTER 12

VALENTINE'S DAY

I believe that summer 1980 was when I became an "obvious" schizophrenic. But even as the spring 1980 semester was ushered in, I was already beginning to have delusions in a broad sense of the word. The "I'm an important person" attitude had begun already, but on the saner side, I felt that I had somehow triumphed over an impossible line-up of courses in fall 1979.

I don't know if I thought of myself as a "transfer student"

at Tydings, if that precludes me from being enthusiastic about or familiar with the school. It was a beautiful, proper place, and one thing everyone noticed was a large mall of soft green grass down the middle of the campus. To me, it sometimes seemed almost as big as the other, more well-known mall in downtown D.C.

I'd often have to walk from one building to the next very briskly. They gave us ten minutes between classes, but sometimes that just wasn't enough. No time to stop and chat. So I was "self-absorbed" on those brisk walks, which might be a clearer way of saying I was stuck inside my own head. I wouldn't have had much to say to anyone anyhow, since I was thinking, constantly thinking about "What's there to deal with next?"

The spring 1980 semester had all the makings of a colorful story, how I was going to triumph over all adversity, how I would neutralize the difficulty of each course by being prepared. So I pretty well positioned the next authority figure not to mess with my mind. That I later let Professor Collins snag me in his "web" I can chalk up to my being a weak person who was not looking out for myself.

The struggle for Malcom Collins was surviving the cut of assistant professors making it to the "associate professor" level—in other words, getting "tenure." How convenient it was to him that I came along. Whether he and his buddy economics professors definitely used me as part of a plan, I'm more sure of as the years go by. I've probably had too much time to think about it though.

And am I "crazy" now? Well, that's debatable. I know the medicine I take erases the delusions, but still leaves me to struggle with my paranoia. Most of the time I try to keep that neutral as well, but even today I cringe when I look at the college catalog list of faculty members. A long time ago he became a "full" professor. Did he deserve it? I don't know. I know he was intelligent.

But life goes on, as it did back then. There in the beginning of 1980, an obvious problem was my sense of self-importance, that feeling of having "good kharma" that overshadowed the extreme paranoia that would surface later before I got on anti-psychotics.

About grades, instead of just leaving my fate up to the teacher, I sometimes lobbied for myself in any course where I felt I might not get an A. In some cases I even asked for leniency. Once, I felt that I had let the teacher think that I would be happy with only a B. When that grade came back in the self-addressed stamped envelope, I knew I had undermined myself when I asked, "Am I going to get a C?" That lesson learned: Be optimistic around teachers.

I still had a "crush" on Professor Brown back at Matthews University in Phoenix. (As ridiculous as that sounds.) I sometimes reflected on what I would say in a letter that he had "asked me to write" by saying to me, "Let me know how everything works out." I gave that statement so much significance. But I was not proud of my performance at Tydings thus far, and put off writing until I could tell him something "big." That something would happen soon.

Todd was the one who asked me to check into the economics honors program at the school. I guess he thought I could push myself even harder. The bigger the challenge the better, he always thought, and I believed it. I spoke with a few of the graduate students who discouraged me, saying the honors program was extra work for nothing. But Professor Welding, who had given me an A in his micro economics course, said I would probably do well. He signed off on a recommendation so I could sign up. This from the man who later said "You're biting off more than you can chew."

I did sign up, even though my understanding of what was involved was murky. I knew I had to have high grades, but wasn't fully aware of the academic elitism in the economics department. Everybody seemed to be protecting their reputations as being "brilliant" if possible. So long to fall 1979 and the simpler ways of getting good grades.

Instead of withdrawing from my intensity at college, as I should have, I didn't back down from my curiosity about the "honors" program, And even though I was an older, returning student, I went ahead and added more pressure on myself by registering for the economics honors seminar class. That would prove to be a disastrous move—maybe even a symptom of my chemical imbalance.

The Spring semester 1980 was just as difficult as the previous one, except I was now in a much different sort of class than I ever had before. It was a first time experience—being in a class where assorted economics professors presented their current research topic every week to a captive audience of about 12 or 13 "honors students." This was supposed to inspire us to select two of the ideas as the starting point for two term papers. Such a perfect situation for someone on the prowl.

And though I stood out as the old married lady, I was thoroughly enjoying myself. It was like a showcase of economics professors. How ideal. The class allowed for much independence, and of course I was overly attentive. That class would require the hardest two papers I would ever attempt to write. Actually, it was the beginning of me making a fool of myself.

I was also taking five other classes, and those were also strenuous. My biggest challenge was to try to understand statistics, my most difficult subject of all. I tried to efficiently manage my academic efforts. A student in the honors seminar class asked me once what I was trying to prove. I always said that I was there for the learning. But who knows what I was thinking as I pushed forward?

I began to imagine that I was an integral part of the economics department at Tydings. There I thought that anyone of importance tried their hardest and that classes were capsules of insight with professors full of theories to explain it all. Something like that.

Add to that an "undergraduate economics club," where students came in the evening to listen to even more "research theory" from economics professors, and you had that kind of viewpoint ad nauseam. Most of the students who attended these talks were the same ones who were considered honors students. The talks were fun to listen to and the comments from the small audience were interesting but mostly above my head.

The whole thing was one more example of a very unearned conceit for me. Sometimes I would heckle the speakers, especially if they were right wing. One professor, talking pro-defense spending, stopped his talk to ask me where he had seen me before. I said the honors seminar class. And he then whispered, "Oh yes, of course."

One risky aspect of the economics club meetings was that alcoholic drinks were served, and I certainly enjoyed that. I thought I noticed whispering, though, one time when a few students saw me drinking sherry fairly late in the evening even as I talked about having a math exam the next morning. They couldn't have imagined what was yet to come.

The whole time with all of that extra-curricular activity, I was still taking <u>five</u> semi-different economics courses. And I was still writing everything down in every class. That semester I had all of my usual eccentricities. My whole life blended together in my many activities, and as usual I was letting the "big picture" at Tydings sink in, deciding how to act.

Then came the momentous encounter—Valentine's Day of 1980—with the seminar class beginning in ten minutes. As usual, I was sitting in front of one of Grammer Hall's plaster pillars, waiting for time to pass. I saw the class teacher, Professor Corcoran walk by with another man. I didn't even bother to look into their faces. In a few minutes, I went into the classroom. Corcoran was introducing that week's speaker.

"Assistant Professor Malcom Collins: A bachelor's degree from Northwestern University, a PhD. from The University of Chicago...a nationally recognized expert in labor economics, his latest research topic is information economics as it relates to employment versus leisure time."

Collins was the first presenter to broach the subject of challenging economics in its use of unrealistic assumptions, such as perfect information. I had heard this alluded to several times by then in other classes, but thought this specific application sounded innovative. At least that's what I told myself.

I found myself intrigued by him, and when I paused to look up, a student named Erin asked him a question: "So what are you trying to say?" I never liked Erin, she had always been so beyond reproach in all of her "higher knowledge." So when Professor Collins gave her a glance down his nose before his short answer, I became interested.

Although he was heavy, there was a certain aristocratic air about him. I thought about Professor Brown back at Matthews University. What would he think about me using this man's research? In a way, they both held labor economics up as their special area of interest. So I was sold.

All of my pushing forward after my return to college must have been to find a situation like this. I just stared at Collins, forgetting for the first time in four semesters to write down what the teacher was saying. Months later I would think it significant that I "met him" there in honors seminar on Valentine's Day. And I thought and always remembered that after he answered Erin's question that day, he looked at me and smiled. In future psychotic breaks I would think he must have been "signaling" me that I was the object of his desire. It really sounds too stupid to write down. My borderline infatuation started there while listening to the young Collins, who was probably the same age as me. I thought he had an unorthodox piece of research in his field, and I decided that his presentation would be the subject I based my first paper on. Unlike the other speakers in that class, he handed out a list of possible topics that the students could pick from. I thought they were all well conceived. Plus that made the assignment a lot easier. I was always bad at picking out topics.

The next day, I had a meeting with a few members of the economics club. At that time, I made a comment about how "handsome" Professor Collins was. I realized my slip-up immediately and followed it with an "I shouldn't say things like that—I'm married." Some of the honors students were friendly towards the young assistant professors, and I thought my comments probably got back to him. Or maybe he had even heard about me before the class—heard it through other sources. But I now had somebody new to worship. Though I didn't think I could forget about Professor Brown from Matthews, I thought taking an assignment from this professor would be a lot of fun.

About a week after his talk, I went to the graduate library to do research for some class. That's where I next saw Professor Collins, making copies and looking great, I thought, in his tailored black coat. Now was my chance to tell him that I was going to use one of his suggested topics as the basis for my first honors seminar paper.

I even had the page he had handed out and started to comment on it. He looked askance at me and said, "Good." I asked how I would look up the journal articles. He said to follow him as we swept down the staircase to the right floor. He grabbed a notebook and showed me what to look for. I watched his hands looking up the correct spot. After that was done, I asked if I could ask him any questions if I got stuck. He said that would be OK.

I was mesmerized and walked around the library with an effervescent attitude. The two journal articles were the best information I had from which to write my paper, since I had been too "busy" to take notes in that class on Valentine's Day. How ironic. The time when I would need good notes the most in my whole college career, I forget to write them down.

I was even more flirtatious this time than with Professor Brown at Matthews. Behind the flirtations was always the promise that there was an "enthusiastic student" underneath the facade. With Collins, I seemed to have grabbed a bit of brilliance and insight without thinking about the consequences. But I still had Professor Brown on my mind, thinking about the letter I was supposed to write about how things had turned out. And I did.

I decided that now was my chance—I certainly had something big to discuss—that I had found a niche in economics and would be working with this young upstart assistant professor on a subject which was certainly going to be difficult. I also told Dr. Brown that he had been the "inspiration" behind my high achievement in the field. Of course, I added that I had become an honors candidate with the department of economics at Tydings.

Years later in December 1982, when we moved back to Phoenix when I was pregnant with Philip, Professor Brown became Todd's masters degree advisor. When Todd first talked to him after moving back, Prof. Brown was sitting on the edge of his chair, Todd said, and asked delicately. "And how did things go for Anne?" Chances are he might have been surprised that Todd and I were still married.

I was ready with some questions for Professor Collins fairly soon after starting my research for the paper. Importantly, I should add, I really did have actual economics questions. By now it seems obvious that I was a flirt, but it was always with the thought in my mind that it would be a "pretend" type of thing with all these "objects of my desire." If anything had happened sexually, that would have so compounded the problem at hand as to make it an incurable mess. But it was always there with me as a "coy" possibility.

In fact, when Professor Kelton, the undergraduate advisor who had stuck me with that killer line-up, was talking to me the very first time later in fall semester 1980 about the Professor Collins saga, his very first question was a hushed and hurried, "Did anything happen?"

But for me I'm not sure if I ever knew what I would do if somebody had actually "hit on me," for lack of a better term. I had to have learned after that New Orleans dance in the hotel room, or a thousand different times I had been a "tease" you could almost say, I should have thought the whole thing out sooner than later. But I didn't, of course, and there I went. Waltzing through this incredibly technical complexion of mens' lives. Did I ever stop to think, well what about if he was married. Why didn't I find that out first? Or actually maybe I was such a sentimental fool I thought "love at first sight" was always a factor.

The funny part is that I really was a serious student. Overwhelmingly so, in my own way.

There in spring 1980, I felt strange that the two journal articles were all I had outside of my knowledge of the principles of economics to write this paper. My whole cover had been blown away. Once again, it's unfortunate that I hadn't taken notes when professor Collins was talking and using the blackboard to prove his economic story line.

I was truly fascinated, because all the "assumptions" that are drummed into the econ student's brain when dealing with graphs or mathematical formula, always perfect competition and perfect information were assumed. And of course all of what he said made perfect sense. I was amazed and inspired, and also taken aback with his intriguing looks and outlook on life. I was like an elementary school student with a crush on the teacher.

I handled my first paper very well, with some help from Collins, who of course wasn't really one of my teachers. I went into his office at least two times in preparation for my first draft. Both times he had me close the door. His secretary gave me sideways glances both times.

And the electricity in the air was invigorating. And he was helpful without really telling me how to go about writing what was pertinent. And our plan was to have me actually do all the work on my own, to prove myself. However, one windfall for me was that he agreed to read my paper before I handed it in for a grade.

Once that happened, he let me know very astutely that I was missing a point from the theory, and should think hard about it. I did, for two days. It really was just a "principles of economics" detail that I had left out, not the information theory. But it was an involved thing to think all of it through to the end of the argument. Maybe even the heart of the argument. The one really impressive paper I wrote during my college career. A few days later and while getting a cup of coffee, I ran into Collins. I told him that I was pretty sure I had figured out what I had done wrong. He smiled and said "Great." I turned it in to him a day later. That bothered my honors seminar teacher who said he should be the one to grade it. He was suspicious about the situation with me and Malcom Collins consulting each other about my school work. I had even named Collins as an "advisor." In any case, they both gave me an A on that assignment. And I deserved it. Of course, I no longer even know in 2000 what that one important detail was. So my one "cerebral" insight in that other assignment is lost.

Along the same lines of trying to impress people, it wasn't just that I was inspired by economics professors; but math and statistics were integral to understanding the economics—and were my toughest subjects to absorb. Later, I mentioned to my calculus professor that my next paper for seminar would discuss a mathematical concept he had covered in his class about the "social diffusion curve." He said he would be glad to help me, though I didn't ask, figuring a department chairman would not have the time.

I had also brought up that proposed subject to Professor Corcoran, who took the seminar class for a beer at the university pub one evening. He had said something that mathematically precise might be accomplished in just one page. It would be impressive. I think he was trying to convince me to untie myself from the Collins gravy train, but I disappointed several people with my very own unethical behavior, and plenty of it.

I went in to see Collins a few days later, after I had settled on the calculus/economics question with the social diffusion curve. He made the comment "I hate 'throwing water' on your idea, but that has already been done." I would later think about him discouraging me in that way, and how unfortunate that relationship and study would turn out, especially from an educational viewpoint. Nobody was being productive with the Bergeron/Collins equation. And what a lousy thing to say to some (by then) senior in college that something has "already been done." So what? Not by me. But I know he had his plans. And I had some transparent plans myself.

So the student/teacher relationship was not all that kosher with me and Professor Collins, safe to say in hindsight. But at the time, I thought that this impressive professor thought that I had what it takes to make new insights into the science of economics. My second paper for Honors Seminar turned out to be: "How Students Maximize their Utility in their Choice of Professors." I thought later that it was obviously a setup for a fall provided by Professor Collins. I no doubt was a laughing stock.

One of my ex-teachers even said, "I was glad to hear you're in the honors program, but why are you doing this?"

I hadn't had economics "utility theory" yet, which covers how consumers maximize their enjoyment of things that are intangibly attractive or obviously profitable—to a point. I'm still not sure if I really understand how it works in the real world with real people. I don't think it's good to ever go around with that intention of maximizing "utility." It's too selfish.

In any case, Collins knew this and more from all of our chatting together. So I was partly dependent on help from him. I thought at the time that he had planned it that way. He gave me a book on consumer theory and told me not to mark it up in any way. Writing that second paper would turn out to be a huge problem for me. And maybe I deserved that. But ultimately I got a reluctant Professor Corcoran to give me an extension beyond my deadline. With the date for that paper put off for a while, I spent time with my other classes. I felt a lot of goodwill from Dr. Corcoran and thought that he knew I was telling the truth about not having the time. For one thing, he was expecting the mathematical paper, thought it sounded "concise."

Collins had told me to come back to remind him once it was summer that he was going to help me out on the paper. Now all three honors courses would be about that subject of labor economics. Prof. Corcoran thought that sounded wise since I was firm in my plans to graduate with honors that next fall semester 1980 by taking both independent honors study and honors thesis at the same time.

As usual, I was asking too much of myself to be able to have any peace of mind. My viewpoint was narrow, partly because I had decided to go to the Tydings "graduate school" of economics to pursue my chosen field after graduation. And I had no intention of dropping my undergraduate thesis debacle. I felt like a significant part of Tydings University, even that I was a well-known student; like in high school, where most people wrote in my senior yearbook that I was a "hard worker." What more could they say?

In college, it was more of the same: "Yes, you worked very hard and got very high grades—what comes after that?" For most professors involved in my returning to college effort, I was no doubt just another student, maybe one who was acting a bit chaotic, but just some student nevertheless. But nobody could have imagined how extreme I was on myself.

As an aside, I liked the idea that the subject of economics could be considered a "behavioral science," the kind of topic I liked and was good at. In fact, I knew this was why Tydings had the economics department in the college of liberal arts. That was the bachelor's degree I was proud of for some reason; whereas at Matthews, economics had been in the college of business.

At the end of spring semester 1980, though, I was intent upon wrapping up my five courses. I still hated statistics and didn't really learn it either. I was glad when that was all over. There was the history of economics, where I went in to the elderly professor's office to tell him I needed an A because I was an honors student. For some reason I also mentioned that my husband worked for the federal government, and I said they read newspapers all day. The professor had replied, "The government employees that I know work very hard."

But I got a well-deserved A in that course. Students in there got together at one point to discuss how to ace the tests. One student memorized the facts in the book which the teacher had written, but still got a B. I knew that writing everything down that was presented in class was the key to success—and I was right. I let some of the other students read my study sheets, and it really did improve their test grades. That's how that semester ended.

But something much stranger in my life was happening, I was getting a huge bald spot on my scalp. I decided to seek out a doctor at the university, and might have discovered my psychotic tendencies right there, if I had listened to the doctor after he looked at my hair. He asked me "Could it be stress?" I told him that my husband and I were just cordial to each other and that I was interested in an assistant professor who "didn't know." He told me to let Collins know how I felt, to take off my wedding ring since there wasn't really a marriage. He said that Todd and I should separate "before you start hating one another." The general practitioner had no way of knowing anything else about my life than what I had told him. He considered me normal, which in a strange sense was true. Yet I had literally pulled my hair out. I was in such a state and nobody knew why. But I left the doctor's office with a kind of excitement about what was going to happen next.

I had liked some of the doctor's ideas, though when he said I should go check with the campus psychiatrist to check my stress level, I just stopped in there for a few minutes, leaving after finding out that I would have to wait 20 minutes. I had already missed some parts of my two favorite soap operas. Looking back I'm ashamed that I ever put watching soap operas before anything.

But the next day I took off my wedding band which had been my mother's. I stayed with Todd though, as he was someone I always needed.

The whole time all of this extracurricular activity was going on, I was still being a super fact absorber. In calculus, I had to take a test which combined math with Basic programming. That was stressful. In fact, the night before that final exam was when I was heckling one of the conservative econ professors at the economics club gathering because he was right-wing. And other big pushes by me were going on for vocational psychology and labor economics. I was already over-saturated, though I dared not tell anyone, not even Todd.

Towards the end of the Spring 1980 semester, Todd and I went to show his mother the campus from the top of a hill near the graduate library. I asked them to wait for 20 minutes while I sought out Professor Collins, for whatever reason. I walked very fast towards his Grammer Hall office, and ran into him while he was rushing in the other direction. He told me he would be glad to help me, but not just then.

Years later, I saw that incident as very significant, like Collins knew Todd and my mother-in-law were there, and thought "How could Anne be pretending to be his wife?" Of course that was paranoia speaking. He was probably just busy with the things professors are busy with.

His disregard for me that day should have given me another hint. I watched him breeze by me more than one time that semester, and had been happy about our fate of having "found each other" for whatever reason God had in store. I was nuts.

Along those same lines, Malcom pointed out twice before the summer sessions 1980 that he knew a woman professor who was much more knowledgeable about labor economics than him. I told him on both occasions that I wanted to use his presentation as the basis of my honors paper, not some other person's ideas. This no doubt helped bring about the very non-academic activity of that summer by <u>both</u> of us. I had asked to go along for the ride, and for that privilege, I would have to compromise myself for the sake of a really ill-conceived infatuation.

CHAPTER 13

PROFESSORS AND CLASS SIZE

Looking back, after Malcom Collins told me the woman professor would be much more appropriate to work with me, I once again blew my cover. I came up with some excuse not to switch over, some way to say, "No, I want to work with you. You are much more familiar with my work. She wouldn't understand." Well, I might as well have shouted my adulation at the top of my lungs for as obvious as I was coming on to him.

He approached me one day after I had called him over in the well of the liberal arts building. He was a big man, a big stomach between us. He said, "Do you know what you're getting into?" And I was thinking of the two-edged sword. Yes, it's a tough subject, but it will be fun working with this guy. I may have at the back of my mind thought, well maybe he's talking about "us," him having the door closed and trying to back off, and me so obviously wanting him. I simply said, "Yes." There you have it.

The actual D-DAY scenerio had been set for the day summer school started. I was supposed to go to his office to discuss the "thesis" I was going to write to graduate with departmental honors. We were going to bat about ideas together. We had been toying with the idea of the "choosing professors" lunacy that I still thought was real.

If somebody had told me I was in the grip of a devious plot developing slowly but surely, I might have thought that was impressive, since it was just me, an older, transfer student. My reasoning powers were off kilter. I knew Collins was considered "brilliant," so I found him irresistible. But then again, probably even for me it was only a mind game. If anything had ever happened between us, I can imagine the delusions that would have been in my mind compared with those that came about from my just flirting with some labor economics guru.

For the first summer school session I had chosen International Economics and Design—both hard courses. Then when we were going to start our brainstorming together and I would go to his office after Design every day. Sounded good to me. But there I was, obsessing about school to put it mildly, skirting the sexual attraction issue while at the same time being drawn into it.

The day we were supposed to start "working together" was set at June 8, 1980, that would give me plenty of time. How do students choose professors? I thought it was a compelling subject. In any case, I wore a jeans skirt and nylons and a gold colored eyelet shirt with little holes in it. I was ready for something; I had imagined it all in my mind. I always thought that game was fun. Flirting, being a tease; it was nothing new. And I think Collins knew it too. I noticed the international economics teacher, Meg, a Ph.D. candidate, glancing at my get-up at one point during class that day. Maybe she too figured out that day would be "special."

At one point later that summer I complained to her that Collins had promised help he hadn't delivered and she said to me "I don't want to hear anything about that."

But there I stood after my two classes, near the elevator, smoking a cigarette. Amusingly, Malcom breezed by and had a quick look my way. He was wearing blue jeans of all things. The only time he ever did. And he wasn't a teacher of anything that summer. That played in well too. He said quickly, "Just give me a few minutes." And so I did. I never minded being given time to think and smoke at the same time. That was one of my specialties. Anyway, I saw him going up the elevator and I soon followed. As usual, I sat in a chair in front of his desk.

Once again, he asked me to close the door. I had gotten used to that. Then he asked me to come sit in a chair to the side of his desk. There it would be "easier" to show me what he was writing down. He was always staring at me, so I should have probably seen what was coming up next. So we started brainstorming about the different qualities of professors almost as if they were products. It was pretty bizzare. Then he mentioned what happened when you saw a full classroom on the first day of school. Of course, that teacher must be "popular."

And on and on we went; it was ridiculous. Yes he could be an easy grader or very knowledgable (Malcom liked that one), or students might even find the teacher "entertaining." There we were in a ridiculous conversation about these "products" called teachers or professors. Not to mention that that whole line of discussion went on all summer. But that was then and this is now. It's all clear looking back in hindsight.

And then the golden nugget arrived: He asked "What about class size as a 'market signal'?" (A buzzword from his specific research area.) Students would use that factor as an indicator of different qualities of the teacher in a given course and class and go from there. "Nobody had ever done that." What would you assume? It had to be something that was quantitative of course. Good old economics. That was one thing we were both thinking about, but we were also thinking about something entirely different.

He drew a simple supply and demand graph on a piece of paper. He said "Look." And I did. Then he said, "Why don't you come closer so you can really understand." And I did. It was just an elementary picture seen often in beginning economics courses. Then he said, "This is how it would look, and it would be impressive." I countered with, "What is some undergraduate doing coming up with new theory?" He said, "That depends." The whole time I was leaning over and he was leaning over, I was thinking, "Shit. What if he tries to kiss me?"

Then after the "That depends," there was a knock on his office door. Malcom said "Come in." Well, it was a graduate student and there we both were, inches apart, on the edge of something obviously sexual. I leaned my chair back to where it was before, embarrassed. Then Malcom turned his full attention to me as soon as the door was shut. He leaned back in his chair, his two hands clasped behind the back of his head. And he looked down, asking me silently to look at him too. There he was, all erect inside those blue jeans. Yes, class size might be impressive I thought, years later. But at that point I didn't get it. Why I was so shocked right then I don't know.

Well I was frozen in my seat. What the hell was I supposed to do then? I made the very sudden and sensible decision to quickly ignore the whole thing. I looked down in my lap until he moved himself back in his chair. I could barely look at him. We were both embarrassed. I quickly said something about what book would be helpful, and he stood up to get something out of his bookcase, but I looked him in the face and he sat down immediately.

I stood up. "Well, I guess I better go and read about all of this theory." I leaned over to get my books and spiral notebooks. I had xeroxed the whole book "Labor Markets." It sat on top of my books. He said, "You haven't read that yet?" and I said no. That was all that it came to. I walked over to the closed door and said, "See you tomorrow" as I left.

Now what I did next is important—just walking out of his office with a bounce in my step, I felt an inappropriate sense of optimism. While I should have felt humiliated, I thought hey the guy likes me too. But I was in a lose-lose situation. I obviously could have moved things forward, but once again I thought of Todd. When I look back to then and then 26 years later with Todd, I'd say we've weathered some tough times.

Everybody would say later that I "had no chance. If you had just gone to Professor Kelton right after that, maybe we'd believe you" said one friend/student much later in fall 1980 after so much more would have transpired. Another student said, "When a man does that to a woman, it just shows…" And then she left. So I never heard her through. I've often tried to analyze what it meant, so many of my actions were based on that.

Anne Bergeron

The route I took through college must have seemed predictable to my friends. I had been in awe of professors since my return to school, usually being a serious student for some male teacher in a position to give me good grades. I had brought that phenomenon with me from Phoenix. And now look what had happened.

As soon as finals were over for Spring, I had assessed where I was going as regards my degree since I was facing four courses in summer school. I had never before been in that intense, same-classes-every-day atmosphere. I had taken advice from Professor Collins about how "difficult" my classes should be for the rest of my time as an undergraduate, so I had signed up for a senior level economics course in both sessions.

I was always concerned about "what the economics department would think" about me taking certain courses, what they would be looking for in their decision on whether to admit me to graduate school. One sinister aspect of Collins' behavior was that he tried to undermine my enthusiasm about academics and learning, which was still there, in spite of some of my motives. Almost everyone who knows I took 45 credit hours of mostly upper-level economics realizes I had a bad advisor.

All of those 400-level courses just took up an extreme amount of time and effort, and Malcom knew that too. Not to mention the "no descriptive statistics" rule he held to so stubbornly. No mean, medium, mode, etc. That's what my study was about! He gave me a list of statistics I could use. Some of them were: factor analysis, analysis of variance, multiple and simple regression, correlation analysis or any kind of other complex statistic that Malcom wanted me to "use in my analysis" amd talk about that summer. And he knew statistics was my weak point. Another unfortunate byproduct of that unseemly relationship.

When Collins and I discussed "students choosing professors" originally, he said that subject would be one way of thinking about labor economics. He added, "I don't know your situation, so it could be questions you can ask customers at a grocery store or some other topic." Who knows what that means, but I suppose that was my chance to be up front about being married and so forth.

Maybe that scene in Malcom's office wouldn't have happened if I had just been honest up front. But the same goes for Collins. He was so damned mysterious about everything, and I was such a fool for going for it.

I can't really say I was "sexually" harrassed, or know if that's possible when you're infatuated and flirting with someone. But there was an environment I should have run away from rather than toward. That aspect of it, him always staring at me and all that summer when I would bring up class size, Collins would flash a quick look at my body, obvious as that was—but just a silent thing between two people. But I know I never again looked at him quite the same after that scene.

But I do believe I was harrassed "educationally," because of his fraudulent personality and his severe and mentally dangerous advice about school. That's about all I worry about with him.

It is like with Anita Hill in 1992. She had stayed "friends" with Clarence Thomas, and the worst thing he had said was something about a "long dong" to her. Or a pubic hair on a coke can, etc. My inappropriate visit with Malcom on June 8, 1980 was of course a lot less strong than it could have been. Just think about it. But it was there, "in the air," and I felt elated and humiliated at the same time. And I've had that problem my whole life. I'd had a disastrous list of boyfriends—up until I met Todd. There's something to be said about starting out as friends like we did.

But there was an uncanny feeling about the "Assistant Professor Malcom Collins" saga. I really do think there was a plan to help him get tenure by showing how discreet he acted when facing what was essentially an openly admiring woman. When he brought up market signals and grocery stores, that must have been where I was supposed to admit that I was married, but

I didn't. I not only didn't react to his suggestion, but I played with the idea, saying "Well, we all go to grocery stores, but I find the academia story more absorbing." (Something like that.)

I left Collins' office after that "discussion," ready for what we had agreed on before the scene. I would come to his office every day after my classes. I got myself primed for a new focus. I bought my textbook and other supplies, and figured out what to wear on my second summer visit to his office.

But now there was this red herring of a dual advance, probably brought on by me. Plus I was getting terrible academic advise from Collins that nearly derailed my graduation from college. What did he want me to do with a move like that? What could any decent person do? One friend later said something about married men having to prove something to their wives. I still don't know what she meant. Maybe I'm simply naive.

And as I said, I thought Meg, my international economics teacher, had looked at me suspiciously that fateful morning. I was "ready" for Collins and felt Meg seemed to know. But of course, I wasn't ready for anything—I was just skirting the edge, trying to be provocative. I would have had trouble convincing the few economics professors I foolishly approached later that what I said about that first summer meeting with Collins was indeed true. I was warned to back off by at least two tenured professors who seemed to know early about the unseemly situation. And I had ignored them.

So on that first day of summer school, when I sat in the chair just across the room in front of Collins' desk, what was I hoping for? There was a predicament there. Maybe it would have been fun bandying around ideas about professors and students. That was our stupid cover, that we were just talking about an "academic" subject. I was just too dense to figure it out, and I was having fun.

What a big-headed idiot he was. What a dumb fool I was. So his other fellow assistant professors who didn't even know me seemed to find our "working together" amusing. Professor

Welding, the father-figure professor from Berkeley asked to see my "results" at one point later that summer. But I had been banned from any kind of simple statistic like Welding might have liked. He must also have been "in on it," I had thought. One of my recurring obsessions was that I always thought I was well-known, even to strangers. Sounds ridiculous, but it's true.

One of the most bizarre things about that summer was that I returned to Collins' office the next day as if nothing had happened. And every day after that, sitting in that same chair next to his desk. But everything had changed. For one thing, it was no longer a closed door situation. At first, he seemed surprised that I was back, and of course I should not have been. Later I thought that he and his buddies might have been trying to show that I was a loose or immoral woman. Definitely not an ideal "honors student."

It was obvious that he was frustrated about my nonchalant attitude from the day before, when he made his overture, and where he had taken that risk of me coming forward. But he probably never thought anything would happen outside of my storming out of his office. I should have realized that Professor Collins had no further intentions of helping me with <u>anything</u> else.

It was probably true that the student who had knocked on the door when Malcom and I were leaning towards each other was there to say I was hanging all over Collins if I had become upset enough to "tell." But I knew I wanted to remain on speaking terms with Malcom, who I thought was a fascinating person. It was fun to pick his brain, and he seemed to think that about me too. Otherwise, why the five hours a week?

I quickly became aware that I was on my own as regards that ill-fated paper on choosing professors. I panicked, not really knowing the theory, and was afraid that because of Collins' temper I was going to do a mediocre job. I called Professor Corcoran at home and said I needed another extension. I told him that "I wasn't getting the help I thought I would from Collins" It was more than a hint that I was being "harassed," since he knew some of the brief history between Collins and I.

That call came after I had brought in some of my second paper for Collins to read one day and he rejected it without even glancing at the first paragraph. He didn't want to see any "writing." So by then, though I didn't figure it out until later, Collins already knew I had "told on him." What a complicated mess I was in. Not wanting to see any "writing or descriptive statistics?" A formula for failure. Or as some say, maybe he was just angry.

Who knows what Malcom and I talked about during those weeks when I was struggling with the "students choosing professors" piece. I should have been angry about Collins' indifference, especially since he had talked me out of writing the much more appropriate mathematics paper with the social diffusion curve from my calculus class. At the very least, that had a potential to be "impressive." But who knows what would have happened then?

But I had my back up against the wall, and should have quickly dumped my entire "departmental honors" efforts. Getting A's in those three classes counted no more than A's in any other classes. Yet they were taking about 90 percent of my studying time.

I had also sought out Professor Welding, an older economics professor who had twice been my teacher and who had signed off on my honors studies application, to tell him (implicitly) about me being manipulated by Collins. But he was a friend of Collins—they were all damned friends. He ended up by telling me "You're biting off more than you can chew." I knew he meant scholasticly as well as regards any problems from Collins. He even told me that he would help me think up a topic to write about for Professor Corcoran. Both of these contacts would come back later to haunt me, since at the beginning of my final semester, both Welding and Corcoran said they remembered my concerns. What in the world had happened that summer? is what they probably thought.

Back in the beginning of summer, though, there was so much more for me to think about than obvious things. I was too busy worrying about what every glance from Collins was supposed to mean, or what Malcom really thought when he said something. To me it was only a thinly veiled, mutual attraction. I was so sure in my mind that he was waiting for me to use his idea so we could start an affair. That's exactly how I read it. And I was always implicit about fending off his desire. Why I didn't think less of him by that point is a mystery. And what must he have thought about me then is probably as someone with an "agenda."

I at first wasn't aware that he had shown his hand and I had folded. The potential was gone, especially after the "not getting the help I thought I'd get" statements (hinting about possible harrassment) about Malcom that I told to both professsors Corcoran and Welding in summer 1980. Oblivious to this, I dropped into Collins' office to chat for an hour every weekday. I guess he could then say just about anything he felt like saying about me. I should at the very least gone back to sitting in the chairs in front of his desk, like most students did. There had been a scene there that I needed to avoid like the plague. I don't know what to say. We all know I was certifiably "crazy".

The summer of 1980 was painfully hot, and the air-conditioner in our house was out of order. And there was life outside of school if you can imagine. Todd and I went to see the Beach Boys at the Washington Monument on the 4th of July. Pictures of my face from that time period show an out-of-control bewilderment. It was true that I was delusional already.

Todd flew back to Milwaukee that summer for his 10-year high school reunion; I dismissed the idea of going with him, or even to my own reunion in Phoenix. I was given a form from my high school on which I was supposed to describe my life briefly, and I wrote, sarcastically: "Tumultuous." It was almost as if I was proud of my predicament.

CHAPTER 14

A BAD IMPRESSION

Going to school each weekday during the summer provided a revealing view of the college on vacation, except for those of us who <u>had to</u> be there. I would never again sign up for a summer class—they were like learning binges. And they were all as hard as any course I ever took.

I was taking International Economics on Professor Collins' advice, just as he had advised for all the economics courses I "just had to take" to get into graduate school. I ended up with 15 courses in economics earned by my graduation in December 1980. Future employers, no matter how fleeting those jobs were, were amazed that I took so much economics. I could and should have been a much more well-rounded student.

That summer, somewhere in between my classes, I had turned in my paper about students choosing professors to Professor Corcoran. All of the different ways I thought up to write that paper had started to confuse me. But I got some economics textbooks from the undergraduate library and taught myself a few of the basics about consumer theory. Also, Malcom had lent me a book about that before the indiscreet incident. I was left to figure out the rest. After reading it, Professor Corcoran gave the paper back to me through Collins, who had the nerve to tell me that I had "fudged" on the paper. I certainly didn't like taking chances like that with my grades. But I squeaked by with an A for that course, whether I deserved it or not. It was lucky for me, since Professor Collins had begun to manipulate me and my college career well before summer session one ever began.

Everything seemed "obvious" to me in 1980, and, as always, I read things into what people said. I knew Collins would look longingly at me, but I thought he was giving me a hint to go ahead and start using his idea. I didn't know what to do about my dangerously small understanding of labor economics.

So Collins and I would discuss the choices that students face, but he still said he "didn't want to see any writing," usually one of my strong points. So we just kept it social, discussing what it was like being a student to me and an assistant professor to him. It was a lot of fun in some ways.

The paranoid but very true thing was that Malcom knew if I were to do any writing or discussing "descriptive statistics" (the only statistics I knew), then I would have nothing to do except talk to him, run off meaningless computer print-outs and ultimately prove his point—this woman is coming on to me. Plus of course he knew with those skills I could actually write the damned thesis. So despite some of my less seemly ways, I still know that he was trying to undermine my college career. That is something I'm sure of to this day, and in certain ways he was successful.

But he asked me why I chose him as my thesis advisor at one point, making some movements with his eyes that I thought meant, "Well, look at my face, I'm obviously young." But I didn't know. He laughed. It was strange that I hadn't looked him up in the catalog on something as important as a line-up of three of my toughest courses. Then I told him I thought he was a visiting professor. He smiled and said "Oh."

So he was more of a roadblock to me than anything else. He wouldn't even be a real teacher of mine until I took his course in the fall. But I was very taken in, and thought that I really wanted him when I really just wanted to influence his mind-set. I wanted to talk to him about himself and how he felt about students. That's what the relationship boiled down to, How do we maximize our utility? For Professor Collins, his behavior seemed mysterious, and I thought there was something more about him that I wanted to understand.

Starting that second day after the "behavior" from him, the door remained open and the flirtation went seemingly unspoken.

He thought it was fun hearing that I thought Professor Welding could at times be completely off-the-wall. Or we enjoyed discussions about grades, with my C in statistics being an "aberration" according to Collins. In a very strange way, we were becoming friends—or at least that's what I thought.

So the first summer session, with me taking Design plus International Economics and all the talking with Collins was unforgettable, to say the least. But when I told Malcom that I wanted to hand out a true/false questionnaire about his idea, I didn't realize how much there was to do. I had to buckle down, having wasted so much time socializing.

There was that Sunday in his office that would happen later, another chance maybe to start a conversation. Collins handed me a black pen I had lent to him, reading aloud, a "Skilcraft—U.S. government" pen. I had another chance to bring up Todd. I paused for a second and then said, "Thanks, that's mine." When it was time to go home, Malcom disappeared down the stairs while I took the elevator. He no doubt knew exactly.

When I had returned home that Sunday in around July of 1980, I felt a little guilty, with my obvious crush on Malcom. Todd was very down to earth when I left, saying "Watch out for yourself." He knew the entire story, because I had told him, although he didn't seem very hurt by it. That might have been quite different if Malcom and I had ever actually <u>done</u> anything. I told Todd about being assigned to write a questionnaire in one day about students choosing professors, and he thought it sounded like a good idea. I even told him what happened with the pen.

Looking back, Todd had always said he had a high opinion of my abilities, even when I was an airhead. I don't know if this was optimism, thinking, hell, she can handle anything, or if he was trying to make me feel better about myself. Or neither.

In later years, even with my unfortunately bad luck in jobs, he always "reminded" me that he had paid a large part of my way through college, and that he didn't necessarily feel that it was all worth it just for the experience of it like I thought it did. In other words, <u>Get a job</u>! That turned out being his mantra over the years, and it's something we've never agreed about since my illness began during my return-to-college days.

Truth is, my life started to take a normal spin in 1991, after no longer working for people who said things about me like "She will be here until she rots." Or no longer having to do anything that required statistical analysis, which was way over my head since my college days. And it is a shame that Todd feels that way, because for almost all of Philip's childhood since then, he has had a very happy mom. There are those who would or would not sympathize with me. It's something impossible to understand for most people.

But in summer 1980, I was going to write up something "significant" that I could test later on the computer. I didn't know exactly how it would work, but decided to stay up all day and night Sunday the day before the second session of summer school, if need be, until the whole thing was done. Since I was in a big rush, I decided to do a survey like you might find in a Cosmopolitan Magazine, like "How Sexy Is Your Love Relationship?" Except mine would ask "What Made You Choose This Class?" It was a big joke, but I didn't know that.

I would test the students on the first day of class to see what information they used to pick the course. Then I would go back after the first exam to see how well they predicted their grades, the interest level of the class, etc. It was fun writing it. I took all day and night Sunday to think up questions and how to ask them, putting out my biggest academic effort ever.

I had not the foggiest idea of how to test for "significance," or use just about any other (to me) complex statistics I would need for the kinds of analysis Collins was bantering about. It was shades of my Economics Statistics class when I got a very lucky C for my efforts. And Collins knew and was friends with that teacher.

In Whose Eyes?
Portrait of a Schizophrenic

It was unfortunate for me that I was working with an assistant professor who did not have my best interests in mind. There was definitely a juncture, if he could only have said, "Forget this departmental honors program and work on getting good grades in your regular classes. That's what's important." I would have listened. Grades were very important to me.

But I thought at the time that "economics honors degree" would look even more impressive on my transcripts than all A's. Instead of quitting the honors endeavor, I was always on the fourth floor of Grammer Hall, "talking to" Professor Collins. And that unsavory period was around July 1980, one year before I first got committed to the mental hospital in Phoenix.

Basically, Collins acted superior towards me once I handed over my finished questionnaire, and I didn't realize that until later. I watched him rush around me as if I was in the way. He probably tried to give me a hint that I shouldn't have still been sitting in that chair on the side of his desk all summer all that time instead of in front of him where most students sat.

Also, I guess I shouldn't have gone through all that trouble of actually creating a questionnaire. I bet the people in charge were just waiting for me to drop out of school after all of the pressure. At least that's what I thought. But they had no idea how stubborn I can be when I have to, or how "intense" I could be. I guess my "worrying problem" began back then.

In any case, Malcom Collins no doubt continued to arrive mornings at his office carrying a handball and a squash racket in his backpack long after I was gone. That's a little of what I thought about years later during my psychotic breaks.

But what was real was that Professor Collins was still putting on his charade late into the summer after he read my questionnaire. He said, "You know you really have something here. Go and sit in this room over here while you think up some questions you forgot to include." This was after he said, "Have you ever heard that senility isn't highly correlated with old age?"

I knew that he meant I should use his idea about class size. That was an "impressive idea," he had said. And basically, why didn't anyone tell me it was a bad idea, how it would be impossible to really test such a thing out? At one point, without even seeing my questionnaires, Professor Welding said if I continued on, my paper would only draw a "C." And he knew how I felt about C's.

More important to me was that this "class size" subject was what we were talking about when the graduate student came into the office back in early June. So I was happy because I believed that Collins was saying, "We're ready to start an affair." Of course, that's only what I presumed to be what he was saying, then and during later "acute" episodes. I just thought I was so smart and savvy, when actually I was just making an idiot of myself. But I had worked very hard in my classes. I really deserved that degree.

That day when I first brought by my questionnaires, while sitting in a tiny room trying to think of how to word the questions about class size, whoever was standing behind me could see my big bald spot—even Malcom. I should have realized that most professors see women staring at them all day in their classrooms. Why I thought I was special was a mystery, though it might have been because I thought I was more "mature" than the average student.

I never saw myself as an over-achiever, simply as right in line with what the graduate economics majors were up to. And I was going to go to graduate school, after all. I never dared to go into the teachers lounge, I just knew I'd better stay away from there. But did I realize what a set of Play Doh I was to the teachers? Not until way later—under duress.

I got so excited about my effort to create a good survey, I even started to think it was "impressive." Professor Collins, though, drew up a chart for me to use to "analyze" my raw data. He wrote down the different statistical methods I could use once I bought my "Statistical Package for the Social Sciences" (SPSS) manual which had statistics even I could figure out. But Collins would have none of the "descriptive statistics," such as average, mode, median that would have been easy to write about. He wanted correlations, simple and multiple regressions, analysis of variance, and factor analysis. It was my most difficult subject, and he knew it. He was a real "joker".

So he condensed those five statistical methods I would be expected to know in graduate school onto one sheet of paper. He also had rows and columns showing "Number of dependent variables" and "Number of independent variables," and so on. People later looked at that list and knew the man was just playing with my lack of insight into statistics. He even knew my two statistics teachers very well.

Apparently, Malcom wanted to be "entertained" by me, just as he thought students wanted to be entertained by their professors. I thought that was one way to think about student choice and class size. One thing that was nice was that the students in the classes I handed out my survey to seemed to enjoy the subject. But it really wasn't a subject to brag about, not even in the most simplistic way. How do collge students choose pens? See—I was back to "marketing." So clever.

After collecting all the two hundred or so questionnaires I had used, I saw Malcom coming up a hill while I was walking down to my car. I waved to him and he came over to see my stack of surveys. He had just broken something to me the day before, when he first saw the handwritten copy of the survey I had designed. It was strange in the way he chose his words. He had snapped at me a few times that morning, but nothing upset me as much as being told to repeat exactly what I had said about the timing of my questionnaire. I asked about a point he was trying to make:

"Yes, you mean that whole thing about my putting this questionnaire off until the last minute?"

"No, the exact statement you made right before you spoke this time." What was he up to, I wondered?

I said, "Umm...I always wait until the last minute to get anything done."

He said, while looking at me, "My wife does that. My wife is a teacher."

My heart just fell; there was such a pain inside me. Right after the wife statement, we took an elevator together and there was complete silence. I had no idea what to say. I thought he was single. He didn't wear a ring. We went into the economics department office to make some xerox copies and I thought, why am I here? I felt the whole room of people looking up from their desks at me, and maybe it was true.

I went home after picking up my things at Collins' office. I felt flushed, embarrassed, in shock. Maybe everyone thought I would give up my honors degree after that, but time was on my side in the summer. I wasn't taking any <u>honors</u> course. And I never would again if given the chance, nor would I ever recommend that anyone in college should. Not worth it, at least not in my case.

I had gone on a drinking binge that night before I handed out my questionnaires to the students. People could tell the next day that I was hung over. I thought, why was he giving me a warning that he was married, if that's what it was? Had I been so obvious? Well we both had. But that statement about "My wife does that (waits until the last second). She's a teacher." was something I would recall in later psychotic breaks as him meaning me as his wife.

In any case, Malcom had come up the hill and over to me on my way home the day after the "wife" bombshell. He was leafing through the completed questionnaires and acted happy to see me. What a cleansing that revelation about being married must have been for him.

But I wanted him to know that I wasn't trying to make any moves on him. This was before I began thinking the two of us were husband and wife—years later. I said, "You know, I'm married too, although my marriage is 'on the rocks'." He said nothing. We walked down towards my car and I started saying, "Well...I'm 28 years old..."

He replied, "I'm older than that;"

"I am a transfer student from Matthews University."

"That's in Phoenix, isn't it?"

"Yes it is." I was hoping that he still wanted more facts about me, like he tried to get that one day when talking about surveys at grocery stores. But I was much too late for that. When we got down to my banged up Pinto station wagon, I said, "I think you have a bad impression about me."

He had a tortured look as he asked, "Why?"

I paused. Should I bring up the obvious? I decided not to. "Well, it's the thing you told Professor Corcoran about me 'fudging' on the test."

The whole scenario was shot. Although we could have gotten close to an actual conversation, Malcom said, "You know I'm only working with you on this project because I see you as an 'enthusiastic student'. If for one minute I thought you had something else in mind, I would drop out as your thesis advisor." I went on, "See what I mean? You think I'm a loose woman."

He countered with, "Where I had a bad impression of you was when we were walking down that hill."

I took the warning well. I decided to stop the exchange. I waved him off with my tortured look. He said something like, "Why don't you go home and get some sleep." I was severely hung over. And probably in all those classes where I had handed out my questions, students and teachers could tell as well.

The confrontation was once again over. He had told me the day before that I would need an SPSS statistical manual. The next morning I went to the bookstore and bought it. I then went to Professor Collins' office and sat in that same chair near his desk. I was not aware of how that must have looked to him. I just know this time he was sure that I would stop coming in, and stop at last from sitting in that side chair.

He looked at me that next day with my brand new manual and said, "Oh…you bought it." As if he was hoping our strange relationship would end. I was feeling fine that morning, not hung over, so I just sat there waiting for his final words for the day.

"I suppose you should start keypunching your data onto computer cards. You can use my account. It's only 'funny money' anyway." Later, I found out that that wasn't true when he showed me the bill months later, with hundreds of dollars racked up by me on his account. Now he was spending money on me.

A whole new era had started. I was in summer session two then, taking Mathematical Economics at 5:00 p.m. in the evenings, every weekday. I continued to go into Collins' office each day at the same time as first session, if you can believe that. And I even tried to let my economics teacher know that I had a connection with Malcom. The teacher said, "I hadn't heard of an Anne Bergeron, though I heard I should be aware of an Erin…" (That Erin.)

So at that hour of the day I was always drunk in time for evening class. That did not go over very well since I needed to read the textbook this time, which was depressing for me. It was the night I was studying for a Mathematical Economics test that I saw a <u>rat</u> in our house at 2:30 a.m. come into my study room under the bottom of the door. It made me hate our house even more.

Looking back on the summer of 1980, it was my prime time for collecting delusions. In fact, even with the one about his "wife" being a teacher, during one psychotic break in the future, I actually started to enroll at Matthews University as an education major. That was very real to me.

But, there were still weeks left in the summer by the time Malcom and I took that walk down the hill. Plenty of time for "analyzing data." I looked forward to our meetings, and made sure I was sober whenever the two of us were to get together during the day. Some things are just hard to understand.

CHAPTER 15

"GO AWAY AND DO YOUR THESIS!"

With all of the times Malcom and I met in his office to discuss "academia" during the summer of 1980, I could have taken two more courses. There were many exits off the runaway train which I could have taken and gotten off. But I waited too long and ended up scarred from the collision with Collins. Certain people said at the end of summer 1980 I looked as if "something very big" had happened to me. What was the matter?

Todd would later say that Malcom had been after "one thing," but I think differently. His interest might have been somewhat sexual at the beginning, but he later seemed just as happy to discuss the subject of my questionnaires as I was. Or so I thought. I guess I truly had "latched onto him" as one teacher later said. But we gave each other the "insider's" point of view. He the teacher and me the student, a multi-faceted topic.

He mislead me badly with the one sheet of "impressive" statistics and no mean, mode, etc.—that was tragic for me. I guess one way of looking at it was that the numbers the correllations and regressions "produced" when plugged into the monster-sized mainframe computer at Tydings did provide for the kind of conversations we always had—strictly general and impersonal. Safe; but I was having fun.

Of course quantitatively I didn't know what I was talking about, and I think Malcom thought that was funny. One thing I've thought about is that the department of economics tried to get me to drop out of college. Maybe that's paranoid, but I think it could be the truth.

I sometimes thought I wanted something sexual from Collins too, but was really afraid of scratching more than just the surface. Of course he could tell a lot about my attitudes just by reading my questionnaires. He gave me one of his research papers to read/admire. I marked it up with colorful highlighters, and of course I thought it was "powerful."

In the time frame from the beginning of summer sessions and fall semester 1980, I even wrote a new "improved" questionnaire, taxing my intellect. And I had made a conscious decision to include two or three questions about class size. I thought of it as part of the flirtation between me and Professor Collins. I imagined the kind of scenario there would be, and talked to Anne G. about everything. Nobody knew that my mentally illness kept getting worse. Unlucky for those who had to deal with me.

I didn't know what was real and what wasn't. I would see the smiles on Collin's friends' faces and think they were laughing at me, that they knew everything. And they probably did. I was no doubt the butt of a few off-colored jokes.

Before the end of summer 1980 Collins told me to steer clear of him for the first two weeks of the fall semester. He said he would be preoccupied. I didn't see that as a problem and went ahead and got ready for school day number one, when a big group of economics students would be reacting to my survey. There I was with a new questionnaire but with no idea as to how to deal with it. I was such an airhead.

One of my former teachers in an "A" class asked me "Why are you doing this?" I told him it was part of the honors program in economics, and he replied, "Well, at least I'm glad that you are in the honors program." In truth, I was just an unfunny joke. And it was really unfair that Malcom used me to get tenure in such a way. But as you will see, nobody believed my story.

My favorite teacher Meg asked me about my survey too. "Did you get help on this?" she asked. When I told her it was Malcom Collins, she seemed suspicious. In any case, Meg was one of the economics teachers there who knew that I was a hard worker and a serious student. I had taken two classes from her. Hopefully she knew that I couldn't have created the questionnaire alone, because it was so inferior statistically and thus somebody had dragged me down. Maybe it was just that obvious.

I also had five new teachers and six classes of my own to think about, and I would be graduating in December. I had my two weeks away from Collins, but then I could stare at him all I wanted to in the course of his that I was now taking. So fall semester 1980 started out mysteriously. Why was everybody asking me about the questionnaire? Even the stalwart, older Professor Welding wondered what had happened with my data from the summer.

And why was I having to steer clear of Malcom? I hadn't heard that he was going anywhere, and he announced his office hours without qualification. As it turned out, it would be enough time for me to miss drop/add and get another class without a "W" for "withdraw" going on my permanent record. And I do believe there were a few academic people who wanted to give me a powerful "censure" for going after a married man.

When I handed out my questionnaires in Professor Collins' class at the beginning of that fall 1980, he left the room for some reason. Intrigued, the students asked me where I had gotten to know him. I told them I knew him from the honors program, that he was my thesis advisor. After class, one of the students commented about how Malcom had lost a lot of weight, and I agreed. I too had been noticing—all summer.

And I wonder what Collins told his "serious" students about "class size." To be honest, I don't think there was an all-around cynicism that went that deep, even among those people who saw unfortunate things happen with me. I think a few people just shook their heads and said it was "too bad" a mental illness had to happen to anyone. I don't think Malcom and his buddies were the type to have those feelings, but I do think from experiencing my life that most people do.

In Malcom's class I was becoming even more infatuated. There I got to see how well the students liked him, and how organized and articulate he could be. Like any good teacher, he

131

liked questions from the class, and when somebody would raise their hand he would look at them and say "Yup?" When one student asked why there was no textbook for the class, he answered "I haven't written it yet." Just as in any teacher's class, I could not bring myself to ask questions. But in between taking notes and other students' questions, I thought I was seeing Malcom stare over at me a lot.

Time passed quickly during those first two weeks. I felt that everything was going my way. I was taking the most "impressive" group of courses that I could, as usual. Unbelievably, I still didn't know what the true "quantitative" elements of my summer efforts were, but I was ready to later go into graduate school, just as Collins had advised. For him to have had me jump through many firey hoops was a sad example of a lack of ethics among faculty. And I wonder if it happens very often at a public university.

I was so happy when my two weeks away from Malcom were up. I had the day all planned out beforehand. After class that day, about two weeks into September, I went up in front of the class when it was over to remind Professor Collins of our "meeting." We agreed on 2:00 p.m., and then I was off to my other classes.

I was so confused, but at the time I thought I was making the right moves. I thought we would agree on a place and time to "get together" when it came right down to it. Again, what would I have done if there was really a "meeting?" I have no idea anymore, though I probably wouldn't have showed up. If I ever see a picture of Collins, that image would no doubt cause some painful feelings in me. I'm no longer quite sure what the guy even looked like.

After a few hours and classes I looked at the clock: it was time. I checked out my appearance in a mirror and went to the elevator, my heart pounding. Then Collins' secretary smiled at me as I entered the office alcove, seeming to know of the appointment between me and Collins. Malcom's first question to me was "Oh, have you finished your thesis?" I said I hadn't. "Well then why are you here?" I almost ignored the question, and amazingly, still sat in "my" seat in his office.

I tried to get a conversation going. He asked me about my thesis and I said, "How could I have finished it without you?" He was looking down on some papers, as if he were doing some grading right then. Was this supposed to be a hint? I'm your teacher now or something along those lines? I would definitely figure that out later. There was an economics book with an impressive title sitting there as if that scene had been previously planned. I would undoubtedly ask about that, certain people probably thought. Being predictable, I did:

"Is this a good book?"

"Oh, this book isn't for you, it's for students in graduate school," he replied. Another hint?

This was at the point where I should have seen a big red light warning me not to go any further. But I didn't.

"The chairman of the department is meeting with all of us in the honors program tomorrow to see what progress we've made," I said.

"Now the chairman is getting involved?" he asked.

"He just wants a brief meeting," I said. I should have known that Collins was well aware of that situation. Since we were back on the subject of my honors studies, I felt I could add: "You know what we've been saying implicitly, 'hinting at' all summer? Well, what do you think now? Can we talk about it?"

"Be explicit," he grumbled.

"You know what I'm talking about."

"Be explicit."

I replied, "But my emotions are involved."

That was the point at which he arose from his seat and started shouting, "Go away and do your thesis!"

I so admired him, but he was so angry. I got scared. "What are you talking about?"

He said, "What you're saying, it's just ludicrous!" Of course everyone in that office area could hear him ward off an immoral woman (or whatever).

"I'm sorry, I'm really sorry," I said, desperately.

"Go away and do your thesis! I remember warning you about this," he said finally. "Just leave."

He was fuming. I felt betrayed and ridiculed.

"You've been playing with my head," I accused him.

"It's you playing games in your head."

I left his office, shaken, going down to the third floor where there was a bench outside of the economics department office. I started whimpering silently. How could this have happened? I felt that I had been "set up for a fall."

But I couldn't sit still for long. My next move to erase the blow-up would be to talk to him on the phone from the graduate library, where nobody would know who he was talking to. Then he could "tell the truth," I thought, about how he was secretly pleased that I finally told the truth about how I felt. I dialed his office. His secretary didn't answer, it was a direct dial. "Malcom, I'm so sorry about the misunderstanding!"

"It wasn't a misunderstanding," he said, glibly.

"I wasn't hitting on you" I moaned.

"Just go away and talk to Dr. Berman (chairman of the economics department) in the morning." He had kept that morsel of information right there in his mind.

I drove home though I was very shaky and depressed. I thought "All of this time it has been him pursuing me, wanting something more than the teacher/student relationship. Now he's acting like <u>he's</u> being harassed!" The whole relationship between the two of us had been extraordinarily unlucky for me. I was still upset that evening when I told Todd about my day.

The next morning was the meeting with Dr. Berman, and I was naive enough to think it really would be about my upcoming thesis. Though he was polite at the beginning, he slowly broke the news to me. "I have spoken with Malcom Collins who told me to relay to you that he does not have enough time this semester to continue on as your thesis advisor. But there will be no time lag at all until you get set up with Professor Connie Wright, who is familiar with this specific study." (The same woman Malcom had discussed with me before.)

I protested right away. "No, you see we had a little misunderstanding yesterday and I'm sure he'll change his mind about this. Also, nobody else would understand these questionnaires."

Dr. Berman advised, "I don't think Malcom Collins is going to change his mind. This year and next are very important to him here at Tydings, you know. He is to have as light a schedule as possible for the next two years so that he can do research in his specific area."

I was upset. "I know you're just lying about Malcom Collins not having the time. I just don't buy it!"

Dr. Berman took a deep breath. "Well you know he actually said that you have a romantic interest in him and he doesn't share that interest in you." Then Berman added, "He is married, you know."

I was just shocked. I thanked Dr. Berman for his time and left for my class with Professor Collins. I caught him as we were entering the classroom. "Professor Collins?" I asked. I thought that would be good, to call him by his full name and title.

He answered, a little unnerved. "I thought you were going to meet with the chairman."

"I already did, I went in early this morning."

For the first time, I sat way in back of the room. Malcom seemed almost giddy, smiling about everything. Years later I would think that was because he knew he had won my love and it was so good to have it out in the open. He was probably just relieved to have a monkey off his back. I would bet that was definitely what was in his "head."

In any case, I tried to talk Malcom out of his decision after class was over. Back near his office, I said, "But you're my inspiration." (How embarrassing.)

He gave me a big smile, but the smile was silent while people only heard the words he was saying. "I will not be your thesis advisor!" What did I expect, that things would go back to the way they were before the confrontation? But Collins wouldn't budge an inch and I left spurned once again.

The strangest drama happened when I went out behind Grammer Hall near the path on which the teachers and graduate students take to the cafeteria the next day. I decided to smoke Collins out. In about ten minutes I saw him walking back towards Grammer Hall with another woman. I glared at Collins, and he noticed me too, maybe thinking I was being comical.

I gave them ten minutes to settle into his office on the fourth floor and then went and approached him again. This time, I sat in the alcove area waiting until the woman sitting in front of him was ready to leave. The woman turned to look towards me and said, "Are you waiting to talk with him?" I just nodded my head. The woman came out to the alcove and traded seats with me. On my way into the office, Collins leaned over his desk top and I could almost hear him saying, "Please let it not be her."

But in I went and started right up. "You're trying to make a fool out of me and embarrass my name, saying I was hitting on you. I know you think I'm a loose woman, but you weren't completely aboveboard yourself." He was just smiling. I continued like this with the woman sitting within earshot. Finally I said, "If you don't become my thesis advisor again, I will tell Dr. Berman how it is I know you were a part of this." (Class size and all.)

The only ray of hope for me came when he said, "I'll have to think about that. Come back tomorrow."

I did wait a whole day, and then he said in no way would he ever be my thesis advisor again. I said, "You probably don't even want me around as a student in your class." He said that wasn't true.

But I had threatened to tell on him and I thought I probably should, even though the man was in a way trapped by the whole thing of me becoming obsessed. I went to Dr. Berman's office, trying to seek revenge. I told him we should shut the door, for our meeting, then spelled out the indiscreet incident with the whole story of Collins' idea about "class size", and our working together that last summer.

Dr. Berman replied, "You don't know what you're saying. Think of the ramifications of this." He didn't go into detail about what those specific words meant, but I looked him in the eyes and said.

"It's true."

Later when I went in to talk with Professor Kelton, he told me, "Now you see what you've brought on yourself?" The day prior, I had broken down and gone in to talk to Kelton, telling him the whole story. His questions were: "Are you in love with him?" and "Who initiated the 'I want to talk about it' statement?" Kelton already knew about the rest. Malcom and I were really tried and found not guilty.

That's not what I thought at the time, though. Of course that would have been an appropriate way to feel; life goes on. Going to Dr. Berman was a big mistake. Though of course something could be done about my graduating that semester. And I do feel that after that some of the teachers and higher ups tried to put roadblocks in my way. I was just lucky that a few things were already signed on the dotted line.

CHAPTER 16

THE DOWNWARD SPIRAL

I may not have had the purest of intentions in all the courses I took, but I deserved most of my grades. And I damned well deserved to graduate with honors for putting up with that crap.

Another thing that happened was that Professor Kelton told me that I needed to get out of Collins' class and into his. He said the last thing I needed was to "stare at Malcom three hours a week." That hurt me because I was enjoying Collins' class and wasn't particularly interested in Kelton's Urban Economics. Not only that, but I didn't have the notes for the first three weeks of Kelton's class lectures.

I borrowed another student's notes, but that experience was never the same as in all of my other courses since returning to college in fall 1978—"owning" the knowledge of each of them because of having all the information written down. Or so I thought. I also hated the "W" I had to take for withdrawing from Collins' class since he purposely waited until the drop/add period was over to start yelling the "Go away and do your thesis" thing. I thought in future psychotic breaks that the day I withdrew I saw him walk on his lunch path with his head bowed, unhappy that I would no longer be in his class.

But at the time what had seemed like such a hopeful last semester for me turned, and the whole world of academia was starting to take its toll on my sense of well-being. I thought I had been framed. Now I was a laughing stock. I still tried to accomplish a lot, but the same verve just wasn't there. One of the students who was in honors seminar the semester before asked me, "What the hell happened to you? You're just not your self." Actually, the summer was all right; it was the confrontation that came two weeks into the fall 1980 semester that had undermined me. There's just no way of aptly describing how I felt at that point in time. My life was a swirl of confusion, malice and betrayal.

There really was a debilitation, since I at that point had fallen apart to the extent that people were noticing the strained look on my face. Professor Corcoran, my former honors seminar teacher, walked up to me just before a statistics class and said, "I hate seeing you this way, I wish I could help." After which I started talking about Malcom Collins and how he would not even be on my "thesis committee" at the end of the semester. I was worrying about irrelevant things.

But that look on my face was not just depression, it was also drunkenness. Add to that my psychosis, and it's amazing I survived that semester at all, let alone with the B's and one A that I got.

Walking into my classes every day became a chore for me. I felt that Malcom's assistant professor friends were laughing at me. They just smiled when they saw me, I felt, and whispered about me to each other. My Public Finance teacher, Professor Rollins, knew a friend of ours and I called him one night at home when I was agitated and wanted him to tell me "What is the true story about Malcom Collins?" He asked me what I meant, but I just said, "Well, between him and me."

He subtly found his way to say he would see me the next day in class, which he did. He came up to me before class to ask if I was all right. I was just so embarrassed. This reinforced the paranoia I was feeling about those professors. The whole departmental honors program had been a complete fiasco for me. I wonder if Todd looks back and feels a little bit guilty for suggesting it. He really shouldn't—it was my final decision.

Then there was Professor Connie Wright, "associate professor," who Collins had wanted me to have as my thesis advisor instead of him. Once I decided to go in and see her, she started in with how I had "latched onto" Malcom and that she would help me only with the specific "class size" study. What was that about? My feelings were hurt when she, one of the two

Independent Honors Studies teachers, whispered to the other one on the first day of class, "I'll take care of this," when she got to my index card of information.

However, once I visited Kelton to tell him about the harrassment, Connie Wright took a different attitude towards me. Kind of a, "Let's see her wriggle over this one." type of sentiment. And now with help from four of her assistant professor friends I really got my head played around with.

I had gotten enthusiastic again when I heard Wright talking about class size. I thought there was some chance that Professor Collins might become involved again, but that was not to be. Being ill already, I thought there were the "sinister aspects" going on in the background. And maybe there were, to some extent anyway.

But a very bizarre situation happened after that. The day I went to the computer center to run off some correlations using my fall study, I had rolled up printouts and was looking forward a little to my meeting with Wright. We had set a time for the meeting. But who was sitting right outside of Professor Wright's office? Four of the assistant professors, including Malcom Collins. They sat around the secretary in perfect silence. They really shook me up being in there like that, and they had to know it would. It was a continuation of the "harassment;" that's how I saw it, and I continue to feel that way even now.

But my paranoia propelled me into totally unchartered territory. How close had I become to all these assistant professors now sitting in a circle with their legs stretched out to intimidate me? It was one of the cruelest things that ever happened to me, even to this day. I guess there were "good ol' boys" in the hierarchy sense there at Tydings University too.

I stepped over the circle of feet that first time they were there, and I had shown up one more time with Collin and his buddies sitting around the little alcove. Finally I gave up on making it to Connie Wright's office to discuss my computer "results." It was always that kind of ridicule thrown my way from the group of Collins' friends there once I had gone to Dr. Kelton. Now, after even having spoken to the chairman about Collins' indiscretion and academic misguidance, I shouldn't have been so surprised at the anger from Malcom and the rest. One problem was that Professor Wright (the woman who would have taken over my thesis) was one of two teachers in my Independent Honors Studies class in my final semester.

One thing that made the whole scene more ridiculous was that "class size," in the literal way, would be impossible to test for. What room number was the teacher on the first day of class? How many chairs were in that room? What was the difference in the level of the class, the size of the room or whether or not it was required, etc. It was so damned humiliating, looking back on it. My first assignment in that honors class was a description of the theory that had created the questionnaire—something Collins had never wanted to see. Why did I include such and such a question? All I had to do was reach inside myself to come up with most of the justifications.

With my thesis, Professor Kelton (undergraduate director of economics) became my new "advisor." He and I had made up the "appropriate" questions to follow up the first questionnaire with. I only ended up having two classes to retest at the proper time, though, since Professor Collins was waiting until after I handed out part two of the questionnaire to have the students in his class take an exam.

I ended up going to Collins' class again anyway, just to show him that life does go on. I could have waited, but Collins would just have waited to give a test too. As it was, he sat on a bench right outside his classroom while I handed out the questionnaires, joined for support by one of his friends. Malcom and I simply glared at each other. Some of the students said, "But we haven't had our test yet." I told them to please fill it out anyway. It was unfair to them too.

Meg wrote on her blackboard before I handed out the follow-up questionnaire in her class, "Anne Bergeron is finishing her thesis. Please cooperate." Professor Welding's Labor Economics class was the other one that worked out for my follow-up questionnaire, probably because Welding was the only other teacher who thought that I might somehow pull it off. And I do think the older Welding from Berkeley was the one tenured professor there who felt bad about what happened to me in that unbelievable year—1980.

While all of this was going on, I was taking one mathematical and five economics courses. What could anyone really say at that point? I remember telling some student about my schedule one day, and he said I should stop with the impossible lineup of classes. He wanted to know my name.

And I also had other things that bothered me in the fall 1980 semester, for example having to wear what Erin pointed out were "plastic shoes," made of burgundy-colored vinyl. I hadn't even thought of that when I was buying them. John Lennon died that year, which was depressing; I got another six pack of beer for that occasion. Erin asked me the next day, "Were you a fan?" It bothered me that my face always showed signs of the night before—drinking, rushing around frantically or not getting any sleep. I would imagine that a lot of people were "fans" of Lennon. But I was there so obviously hung over that some of the honors students actually stopped thinking it was funny. I think they were a little worried about me if that's possible.

The second and last assignment in the independent honors studies was for each of the students to get up in front of the class to show and explain their "thesis" topic. For me, this was doubly important, since I was graduating in a month. Professor Wright and some of the other honors students asked me how I would be able to finish up my thesis in time. I insisted that I would, though Wright said, "Not this semester anyway."

Someone was playing with my fate. It wasn't sexual harrassment, since it was me who was "coming on to" Malcom Collins towards the beginning. But the whole "It's already been done," "Yes take 15 economics courses, "Of course you'll need that at graduate school," the "I don't want to see any writing or descriptive statistics." It's a real shame somebody got away with that. And he got full tenure.

I think the staff at Tydings knew I was going crazy, maybe even knowing it was schizophrenia, and because of that I would be a bad representative of that school as a graduate. I do think I know a lot of the professors felt bad about my evolving in that way, since I was a good student in most of their classes. Who knows what would have happened if I had stayed at Tydings even one more semester.

I remember at the height of the confusion, Professor Welding, who had been a good supporter, again told some of the teachers to tell me I would only get a "C" on the thesis, since I didn't have a large enough "sample size." Later I found out that was ridiculous, rather the topic wouldn't have worked out because of all sorts of technicalities <u>except</u> that one. But by the time all of that came along I was already losing part of my intellect or verve, as I've said. If I had gone another semester I would have been a drop-out, and I don't think the economics department would have felt at all bad about that. Again, I think that's what they hoped would happen.

My presentation to my fellow students was clearly flawed. I drew some diagrams and did some equations to prove some points, but like a friend of ours said the night before when I asked him for advice, "I'm not entirely sure that you know what you're talking about." So that was another embarrassment for my fellow students to see. Maybe they were snickering, but nobody cared enough to jump up and say, "Can't you see what you're doing? A thesis about 'class size'? Don't be ridiculous."

In the second report, I had the other teacher see my computer print-outs and written material about the subject of class size and the rest of the variables. The honors study professor came back with "What are you going to do with all this data?" Just like Dr. Welding had asked. I was still thinking I could get "results" from my questionnaires and "difficult" statistics. (Way above my head.)

With all of what preceded my next move, I should have ruled it <u>out</u>. What was I getting when I tried to get through to Malcom Collins? A brick wall. But in one of my discussions about my thesis, Professor Kelton made one out of context statement to me about Malcom and his "feelings" about me. Now that might have meant fear and loathing, as well as anything else, but I took that statement home with me on a night when Todd wasn't there to bounce ideas off of. I decided that what Kelton said meant that Malcom's "emotions were involved," just like I had said to Collins on the day of the blow-up.

I decided that I needed to write Malcom a letter telling him how people he thought were friends were actually "trying to keep us apart." (Yes, I was crazy.) I said Professor Kelton had told me something that made me happy about how Malcom felt. I pointed out how obvious this was since Connie Wright from UW-Madison had tried to get me to do a study using the subject of "class size."

I continued, "I don't want to talk about this to Professor Welding, or Professor Kelton, or any of the four people who were in that "silent circle of friends" over by Connie Wright's office. I slid the letter under Collins' closed door. I had finished the letter with a, "And I will call you right after Public Finance today (in one hour)." I did, and said, "Do you want to get together?"

Collins said harshly.

"No!"

This shocked me, I thought he would have liked to know about the intentions of his so-called friends. But then I knew I had done something very wrong in giving Collins something in writing. I went up to his office to "get back my letter."

Malcom sneered at me and said.

"I tore that letter up into tiny pieces."

I was walking fast down the hall with him, when I said something about being made a fool of. He ducked into the men's room. Nothing I could say then. I was crushed.

When Professor Kelton found out from me about the letter, he told me to start seeing a psychologist or he would refuse to be my new thesis advisor. He asked, "And what did you say about me?" I told him that the letter pointed out that Kelton had been the one to let me know about Collins "feelings." Later, Kelton visited Collins in his office and said that Collins wouldn't show him the letter. Kelton thought that was "big of him."

Now my fate would be woven into something else by a "psychologist." I needed medication, (hence a psychiatrist) not somebody from a profession that seemed to always need an emotional reason for everything. It was surprising that when I went to talk to that Ph.D. candidate psychologist who taped my sessions each week for forty minutes, he didn't see any hint of schizophrenia. His dissertation advisor also thought that I was just experiencing "anxiety."

Although I went there for almost a month, they didn't come up with anything helpful, in spite of my telling them over and over again about all of my obvious delusions. Before he stopped therapy, once I was graduating, he and his professor/advisor told me I should go and tell the university's provost about the kind of "sexual discrimination" I was facing. They also told me not to graduate then, to strive instead for my honors degree. May 1981 wasn't that far away. Luckily, I rejected both ideas. That Ph.D. student who taped me all those times should have also been rejected as a Ph.D candidate.

The sessions with him were disappointing, and I would run into more problems along those lines with psychologists. It was unfortunate that the person I confided in in fall semester 1980 didn't recognize the "un-reality" of my ideas. Although I had made an honest effort to seek help, his oversight could have cost me my life by July of the following year due to that 38-day fast. I've always remembered that.

Anne Bergeron

Late in fall 1980 at Tydings, there was a lot of activity from me and also from those around me. By that point I thought that there was a plot to keep me from graduating, but I wasn't aware of just how right I was. One very good thing, in fall semester 1979, when I had just transferred from Matthews University, wanted to make sure that my upper-level business courses would qualify for credit during my sign offs of requirements in fall 1980. Professor Welding, the older teacher during that first semester at Tydings, said there would be no problem, with Matthews University being accredited just like they were. But I wrote out a list of them and had him sign it with a note that these courses will count as "related upper-level courses" towards my degree.

When I finally got assigned an "official" advisor in fall 1980, I went to him for his signature of my sign out documents. I let him, a teacher I didn't know, play his hand, and in the end he "wasn't sure" about the miscellaneous courses I was claiming were related to economics. He was definitely told to give me a hard time, or had just decided to do so on his own.

Finally, after an eeiry discussion, I said, "I have a note here from Professor Welding," which I showed him. He seemed relieved. I ran into Welding again that day and he had all ready heard that I had still had my signed note.

I had a few games of my own. Late in my final semester, after I had started to feel "dark," I asked Todd and a friend of ours to come to my classes. In Urban Economics, Todd answered a question about "information economics" for me, which was strange. By the time we were ready for my statistics class, the professor had called off class for that day. I found that very significant. I, Todd and our friend stood out behind Grammer Hall during lunch time, trying to smoke out Professor Collins. Some of his friends walked by, smiling, but he never showed up.

Again, both sides were playing games. My statistics teacher, an assistant professor, told us students to call him if we wanted to go over our test results. I did that and he said, "Well, come on

146

up." He was on the same floor as Malcom. As soon as I got off the elevator, I saw Collins eying me, standing in the hall. That shook me up, and then I asked my statistics teacher if he was a friend of Malcom's. If the answer had been positive, I again would probably have asked what the "real story" was about me and Professor Collins. Instead my statistics teacher said, "Well, I know 'of' him."

At some point late in the fall semester, I found out that somebody had given me an incomplete in Honors Thesis, leaving three hours more that I needed to graduate. My only hope was to get the mathematics department to accept my Intermediate Algebra course from Matthews U., which they had refused to do. But I had been diligent about my graduation and had prepared for just such an occasion.

I had written to the chairman of Matthews' mathematics department to say Tydings was declining to give me transfer credit for that course. Luckily, he had sent a letter back to me, saying it was at this or that level, but if it was accepted at Matthews, Tydings should do the same. When I went in to show the letter to the vice-chairman of the math department, she asked, "Have I seen this letter before?". I said she hadn't.

She left me alone in a classroom while she went to discuss the point with someone, the chairman, perhaps. I decided to stay still the whole time she was gone. After about 25 minutes she came back with a slip of paper accepting the course as a "math elective," and she said, "Some seniors wait until the last minute." But I then had my 120 hours to graduate.

When I brought that slip of paper back to the behavioral science college, I quickly changed the atmosphere surrounding my efforts. In one way at least, I had a lot to celebrate. I was just a few weeks away from being a college graduate and was very excited. The only thing that could have made me happier was if I was graduating "magna cum laude," which would have been possible if it weren't for my last semester. I had spent way too much time being big headed in two honors courses. I was jealous

147

of Erin about her freedom to concentrate on getting good grades in all her courses once she had dropped out of that program. With "departmental honors," I had once again become too worked up. And they made me fight for my grades in two fall semester 1980 classes, since for some reason I ended up having to make points clear to two obviously intelligent professors that I had gotten this or that grade in their courses, just as we had both said. Other insignificant things made me feel bad. In essence, I was too worried about too many things: My paranoia was running rampant, as usual.

After straightening out my grades, I ended back up on the fourth floor. Afterward, I had my back to Malcom's office while I was waiting for a down elevator. But I turned around when I got on. Malcom Collins stood there with a big smile for his secretary, (and I thought for me too) while he said, "We're going to wait." I later thought he meant, "Anne and I are going to wait to get together until the 'right' time." But I knew I would first have to put together all the puzzle pieces. And I remembered those words so many times in future psychotic breaks. And that was the last time I ever saw him.

CHAPTER 17

Ph.D ECONOMISTS

Graduation was about a week away after I had to "derive" my grades from those few teachers. I would be back later in cap and gown. I told people in my family that I wasn't sure if I was really graduating, given that the math elective might not have been recorded. Or that I couldn't graduate with an "incomplete" on my record. In addition, perhaps the authorities thought I didn't deserve to graduate. Of course I was graduating, but I had become used to being unhappy in my last semester and had a hard time letting Tydings go. I had poured so much of myself into it.

In the end, I "felt" that I had graduated, at least I was sure enough to go to the ceremonies dressed up in a cap and gown. And I was in the program. Todd's mother gave me a pretty gold chain and helped me with the stiff white collar. I knew hardly anyone was going to see me graduate, except for my good friend, Anne G., Todd and my mother-in-law and father-in-law.

I saw Dr. Berman, chairman of the economics department, during the preparation for the procession to "Pomp and Circumstance." I didn't look him in the eye, though I knew he saw me. I made sure of that. But I hadn't listened when Todd told me where in the crowd their group would be. I was afraid to look around, too, because I was almost certain Malcom and his friends would be there watching me. So I was just stuck there in the middle of the crowd.

When it came time to walk in line with the music, I headed straight for the College of Behavioral and Social Sciences area on the floor of the Tydings basketball arena. There were people everywhere. As I headed for the back row, I heard Erin whispering loudly, "Anne, come sit with us!" I didn't acknowledge her at all, I didn't even want to know who the rest of "us" was. She had a star near her name for magna cum laude, and I was jealous. I just sat with a few male students from my Public Finance class. When the officials called out for our college, I followed the crowd exactly, doing all the proper things. I was just glad to get out of there.

Afterwards, Todd's mother took three instamatic pictures of me with Todd and two by myself and gave them all to me. Anne G. had left after some hugs and congratulations. She was always such a good friend. Not even two of our best friends, James and Karl, made it. Things had just been so crazy. Later, Todd, his parents and I went out to eat at an Italian restaurant, and we were the only ones there at around 2 p.m.

That same day, we drove down to celebrate Christmas with Todd's parents, brother, sister and brother-in-law in Raleigh, North Carolina. I had the four of them stop at a convenience store to buy a few cans of beer on the way. You could almost hear the pressure building up from my father-in-law, who was in the front seat as usual, and Todd's mother and I, who always had to sit in the back when they were visiting. So there was me, sipping beer within a few inches of Todd's mother, marking time.

Todd and I spent most of that chilly Christmas Eve standing out on Todd's brother's apartment balcony. Todd and his brother-in-law had driven to the store to pick up some more beer, and we were drinking it outside. There was no real connection from those inside to me, except for Todd. They were a little, close-knit group, watching a church service on television while Todd and I finished up a 12-pack out front. We all did get together inside for a ham dinner and opened our one gift from Todd's mother and father.

I woke up the next morning with a severe stomach ache, and went into the kitchen where Todd's brother was waiting. Todd was out front, and told me later that his father had come out and told him "What Anne needs is a swift kick in the ass!" But there

I was, in agony and dumb enough to mention it. This is where my brother-in-law started shouting.

"Well what do you expect the day after you've guzzled a half case of beer." The whole scene was very violent verbally.

Todd's father joined in the shouting match with: "You know there are places you could get help!"

For her part, Todd's mother was just crying, like me, about the noisy scene. Finally, Todd came in, assessed the situation, and said that he and I should leave. We left, but the stomach pain (which I had never had before) continued. It made me wonder a little about food poisoning I was so upset, but maybe it was just that everything had simply built up inside of me. I was doubled over for the whole trip back to D.C.

The next few days back in Washington, I wrote a resume to help me get a job as a research assistant for some consulting firm in the yellow pages. To write it, I remembered what I had learned from a Business Communications course at Matthews University, including the "Objective." I wrote something about how I wanted "some practical experience with economics before continuing on with graduate school."

I got letters from two firms wishing me luck, but a Dr. Hugo Knight from the ICC, Inc. Consulting Firm, actually called me to set up an interview. He met me out front near the elevator. I was surprised at his appearance, almost like a member of the rock group "ZZ Top," with the long beard and so forth. But he brought me back into his office to interview me with his partner at the firm, who looked totally innocuous.

It was about a 15 minute interview, where they asked me about statistics. They gave me a situation and asked me what I would do. I said "I would use some sort of statistic." They said, "Good answer! Now what kind?" And so on. But I squeaked by and was lucky they asked about a method I knew. A rarity. I also mentioned that I wanted to make $15,000 per year and they said they only pay beginners $13,000. Back at home, I wrote Hugo Knight a letter saying that of course money wasn't as important as working for such an impressive company. Within a few days, Dr. Knight called back to offer me a job paying $13,500, and I accepted.

On the first day of work, I was introduced to my supervisor, Dr. Thomas Kramer. He seemed nice, very mellow. Later, Dr. Knight called me to his office. I sat down while he talked about the letter I had sent to him; I had misspelled his name. He pointed out that he hoped this would be the last detail I work with that turns out to be incorrect. He also said to call him Hugo.

Apparently doomed from the start, I got off on entirely the wrong foot at that company. Of course, one of the first things they found out about me was that I smoked cigarettes. So did my officemate, but they were still not pleased. Almost as if even with that I had mislead them.

But my first real faux pas occurred at a goodbye luncheon during my first week for one of the researchers who had been accepted to Stanford graduate school. I didn't know him at all, but presumptuously went to the luncheon and sat in the chair right next to him. Don't ask me why, because I don't know. It was bizarre that I even had the nerve to invite myself.

Hugo made us all change our seats, stashing me away in a corner and continuing the luncheon. I then got to talking with some of the workers there how I looked "younger than my age." In reality, I should have volunteered to stay behind to answer the phones for the secretary at ICC who knew the man could have gone. That was not a good way to start out, to say the least.

Another happenstance was when Todd and I crashed an ensemble at a "Vegi Pub" hosted by Hugo and his partner that I had found out about at the inappropriate luncheon. Hugo came by Todd and me with a few sneers at the two of us drinking beer out of our own glasses. There was supposed to be no alcohol. One more place where I shouldn't have been so soon after getting hired. Or so I assumed after seeing Hugo's reaction.

Right after those two incidences, Hugo started to glare at me when we passed each other in the hall. Thomas Kramer remained fairly nice to me, but even he once told me "Never come to this office again when you're hung over." I began going to the basement of a nearby restaurant to use their bathroom to flood my wild looking eyes with drops every morning. My eyes were filled with tiny red veins, and I felt that the eye solution helped me look more "normal."

Back at the office, I spent my time reading off my lists of numbers to one of the secretaries. Someone there told me that that was a good way of doing miscellaneous proofreading of Lotus 1, 2, 3 type of data. Of course this was a very dense way of checking for accuracy to top off more of this situation. Also, I remembered very little about statistics and needed to have Thomas help me with every single assignment.

But I was used to acting obsessively and made the same moves at ICC. I felt I needed to overdo it there as well, for no apparent reason. When it was time for everyone but the big wigs to go home, I would tell Thomas that I would be staying late to help him out. With what? Once I even came in on a Sunday, and Hugo came up to me and said, "I hope I'm not breaking apart a happy family."

I thought maybe he was talking about Malcom and me in the future, so I said, "I hope not."

He then put a gentle hand on my shoulder, the only time I was ever to see Hugo act personally towards me. A few times during my employment, he could come up and say something meaningful to me, like: "You could try as hard as you can and you would never spend as much time here as I do."

One time they brought Hugo in to see me obviously strung out from the night before. He answered my "How are you?" with a "...And how are you?"

There were even a few times during my three months at ICC that I drank alcohol with some of the other employees. Once Hugo called a meeting and passed champagne around. I went back for a refill two times; nobody else had more than one. Another time was when the others asked me to join them for happy hour at a bar near the office. I used my credit card to buy a round or two for everyone. Todd wasn't there so I tried to maintain my control. I got a ride home with one of the men at the office after I told him I would be riding the subway home, and then I left my purse in his car. I panicked, though I got it back the next day. However, I knew that this friend of Hugo had probably gone through my belongings.

My officemate was nice, but she was tired of my melodrama. A few times I closed our office door so we could discuss my "divorce" from Todd. I probably seemed like an opportunistic and shallow woman. More than a few times I discussed my appearance, saying stuff like, "I know I look strange today, what will Thomas think of the look on my face?"

My officemate said after a while, "What's all this about how you look? I don't need to look good, and I don't care how you look."

I was always staying late, working at things that didn't fit into a "bigger picture." When I wasn't staying late, I was bringing home an armful of work. To do what with who knows? Once, with the latter, Hugo Knight got on the elevator with me:

"Going home early today?" he asked, looking appalled as usual.

"Yes, I try to be normal," I said.

"Is that what you really said, you try to be normal?" asked Hugo. I said it was. There was a silence but I got a chance to say one more thing:

"So how's business going?"

He repeated that one too, still surprised. I could tell he was sorry that he had hired me. My lack of good judgement had been evident on most occasions. I no doubt altered the way people at ICC selected new employees from then on. That happened a lot in my work history.

It's not that I didn't try to understand the statistics they dealt with there, I just never had that type of information down pat. Tom Kramer put some formulas up on his blackboard in his office for me once, but that didn't help either. It was all oblivious to me. The loss of intellect was building up.

One time I sat next to him while he was programming the computer for one of his studies, but outside of being impressed, I took none of it away with me. I had a kind of dependence upon him, as if I could understand statistics only if it was him who taught me. I was such a dweeb sometimes.

After I was with ICC for about a month, Hugo's partner came in one day and asked me if I could meet with a few clients the next day and work on one of their projects with them. I went out and bought myself a very pretty outfit and was ready the next day for something important. All the meeting turned out to be was my working with disgruntled ex-clients who did not at all like the conclusions ICC had come up with regarding a study done for them. Settling the dispute amounted to going over vast amounts of pages and deleting anything pertaining to their biased hiring practices. It was a put down and nobody else had even wanted to talk to them. After that, I refused to have anything to do with the partner who gave me that assignment. Justifiably, in this case.

I also began acting strangely towards the other people I worked with. I knew the secretaries were "gossiping" about me, and that other employees just talked to me for the entertainment value of it. (Which could be true.) I even felt that people were being "sent" into my office for various reasons. This came up later at the county crisis clinic in summer 1981.

One time during a talk with my officemate, Hugo was my target, how he had hired me just to "watch over me" for his friends at the university. Although I didn't come right out and say it, my comments centered on that theme of me not being a "career woman." Another foreshadowing.

I knew I was not suited for what I was doing, and thought perhaps that's why I was there; to keep me busy and "under the wings" of Thomas and Hugo. However, the officemate said no chance Hugo would be that unselfish. I was now paranoid enough to think the people at ICC were making up stories to keep me in the dark. Everything was being done "in secret." Hugo glaring at me whenever we were near each other only enhanced my paranoia.

Ultimately, I even refused to go to Tom Kramer's office when he buzzed me on the intercom. I had started having delusions that people were talking about how I was "hitting on Tom" now. And, vice-versa. Why I thought this is a mystery, because there never was one shred of flirtation from him.

Once I started to refuse to see him, he told me that I was "skating on thin ice." I thought that was funny. In fact, all of my psychoses during that time were cheery, I hadn't yet sat back and realized what was happening to me. I thought that I was just somebody who a lot of things "happened" to. I never realized that having activities by and around me seeming so "significant" to me was abnormal. That goes without saying. I still just figured that I was an important person. More delusions of grandeur.

The other employees had to know I was psychotic: not going to my boss' office when he summoned me; my closed-door and warped discussions with my officemate, etc. My mind was already honing in on the setting of my delusions, the campus at Tydings, and especially the Grammer Building and the summer of 1980. I brought Malcom's research paper to the office to file away for Thomas to see when he "rifled through my files," as he once put it.

While all of this was going on, I was starting to tell Todd that we were "just friends." We had almost daily discussions about our relationship. Todd was always faithful to me, and I was always faithful to him. That's the surprising part. I could really talk a game, but to know somebody else sexually wasn't what I wanted.

One strange aspect of what happened in the spring of 1981 was that Todd was trying to get admitted into Tydings University as a Ph.D. candidate in the field of economics. I thought he would be given a hard time by the economics faculty, but it probably would have just been the opposite. The employees at ICC knew some of this and asked me if I thought I "owed him one" for having paid for my degree. I didn't know what to say, given all the strange "sub-plots" I felt going on around me. So I said something like "I suppose so."

It turned out that Todd was accepted by Tydings by the end of the spring semester before I got fired. And they also offered him a teaching assistantship. He should have gone, but maybe all the confusion lead him to give that opportunity away. It could also have been the state of his career at that time, with people working in the federal government starting to get laid off. He wasn't sure he would be able to get back in if he needed to later.

My confusion deepened. For a short time I thought I might belong with Tom Kramer rather than Malcom Collins. (What about Todd?) At one point I told Todd, "Three strikes you're out—Professor Brown, Professor Collins and now Dr. Kramer." I even started thinking maybe I should get a Ph.D. in statistics for the ultimate challenge. (Dr. Kramer had one.)

At the same time, I was leading the way into getting fired from my job with Hugo and company. Always staying late to do more "analysis," I decided that I couldn't do that any more. I would just hang around Thomas when I stayed, and I thought it was obvious that he had a girlfriend. In fact, I thought "they" even had her come in and work with me one day at the office. I felt the higher-ups thought up that one. Of course, I wasn't really sure, I just "had an inkling" that the woman was Tom's girlfriend.

ICC's marketing director came by to talk to me towards the end of my employment there. She said, "It's a very scary thing, hiring someone." Not very subtle. That was shortly before I got the call that Hugo wanted me to come to his office after work that day. He had me sit in a chair about ten feet in front of him.

"You're starting to scare the other employees." He said, "I've decided to give you two week's pay and ask that you leave us as of today." I had heard of an employee who Hugo had told could take three months to find a new job. The reason he left was because he did "too much socializing," according to the gossip. But he also had worked there over a year.

Hugo said the least negative thing he could to me in justifying my discharge: that I was "too narrowly focused on one issue at a time; transfixed by certain variables and zeroing in only on factual things." Whatever that really meant.

I responded, "So you fired Bill for being too social and you're firing me for not being social enough?" He didn't respond. I told him I was sorry for being so distracted, that there were big issues on the forefront for me and that's why I hadn't thought enough about the big picture. I also told him there was some confusion in my social life outside the office background, that there was a "Mr. X versus a Mr. Y" He said he didn't even want to know about that. But whatever I said, it softened his stance.

"OK, then take this talk as a stern warning that you are under consideration for being fired." He added, "When you came in twenty minutes ago, I would not have predicted any chance of something like this happening, but you have bought yourself some time. I will be watching very carefully." I figured out later that he might have been scared of me himself.

I got the warning on April 30, 1981, the day before I was to move into the apartment that Todd helped me find in D.C. Not long before the predicament with Hugo Knight, I had again told Todd that we were now just friends. I felt it hypocritical of me to continue living in our townhouse, accepting support from him. To this he said, "OK, so you start paying me rent." I said that I would. And he did make me sign something.

At ICC, after Hugo gave me the warning, I went back into my office to think. Tomorrow was moving day. Had they known? I started to cry, mostly for effect. I put in a call to Todd, who was at home. "Please come and get me. I've been fired," I said. This was partly because I was doubtful that I could ever become the kind of employee that Hugo wanted me to be—but I was putting on a show mostly for effect.

He walked by my office on his way out and seemed taken aback by my teary eyed phone conversation. The marketing woman overheard and asked me what had happened. After I told her, she said nobody who had ever been warned survived the warning to stay on. So I decided that maybe I had just put words into Hugo's mouth. It was very confusing.

Minutes later, I went over to Burger King to meet up with Todd. We had a discussion, but he didn't know what to say about my being fired. On some level he was probably a little upset, since ICC was a great place for me to have started working right after graduation. But I was in no position to take advantage of that. I was going downhill at a very quick pace.

I decided that I had saved up enough money to rent the apartment the next day anyway, in spite of my warning. The next day, Todd and I lugged everything into the car, ending up making many trips back and forth for my things. On the first trip over, I met up with my two landlords who were waiting out in front of my new building. I gave them my check and they gave me the keys. They asked about Todd, "Who's that helping you out?"

I said, "That's Todd…He's a friend."

That night, May 1, 1981, I decided to write and give a letter to Hugo the next morning, telling him what's what. I had read the letter to Todd the night before. I started the letter with, "Dear Dr. Knight, alias 'Hugo," and that must have set the tone. I went on to tell him that he didn't have the power to fire me, that the president of the firm had no business going over Thomas Kramer's head to attempt to get rid of me.

I went on and on about how he had been against me from the start, how condescending he could be, and how he was a shallow person. The next day at work, May 2, 1981, I slid the letter into Hugo's mail box and then just went to my desk, as if all was as usual. One thing had changed at least—I had decided not to speak to anyone.

People tried to talk to me, but I decided I couldn't even talk to Tom, my immediate supervisor. He finally said to me, "OK, so you like things down in writing. I'll be back." I was noticing all the movement around me.

The other employees continued talking to me, though they got no response. It probably would have looked comical to outsiders who weren't familiar with my "personality." There I was at my desk, reviewing some data, with my back to everyone. Tom Kramer finally came up with a decision and handed me the letter.

"Obviously, nothing has changed since we spoke on Thursday, the 30th of April, 1981. Please be advised…that your employment with us is now terminated." That was the portion of the letter from Dr. Hugo Knight, president of ICC. Below his signature was another part of the letter:

"I concur with the decision made by Dr. Knight to terminate your employment with ICC." That part was signed by Dr. Thomas Kramer.

Once I read that letter, I knew it was time to leave. I gathered up none of my things, leaving items like Malcom Collins' research paper there for everyone to see, as well as my files for somebody else to organize. Nobody said a word once I had stood up, and I slipped away silently, waiting for the elevator with the letter in point clutched in my hand.

I was on the bus to my new "home" near the zoo. My apartment was just perfect, both Todd and I thought. For one thing, I wouldn't need a car at all.

The rest was critical—the almost dying and movement of belongings. Just where I had landed on May 1, 1981, was debatable. Certainly I was not starting out on my own. I was basically there to play out my fantasies, moving to where I would be most accessible to the people who needed to "come through" for me, such as Malcom Collins and others in my long-running saga. One time I started to tell my officemate at ICC where I was moving to, and she breathed in real quickly, like, now that's a scary thought. I would imagine so.

Of course nobody ever visited my apartment except for Todd the whole time I was there. The whole living by myself thing at that point was a fraud. The little studio apartment was a stage of course. I kept expecting big things to happen, but outside of almost leaving and throwing everything away, nothing did.

I remember calling Hugo about a year and a half later after arriving back in D.C. after my county crisis clinic experience. He got on the phone and said "You were somebody that I thought I would never hear from again." I told him that during my time with ICC I had had some "problems." He said, "Mmm hmm." I asked him if he would ever consider rehiring me, and he said "No, the other employees would remember."

Then about a month after that I called him again. I told him I was going to have to become a secretary again if he didn't rehire me, and for the second time in the whole mental epic I had somebody tell me "It happens to the best of us." Then he said, "Did I ever intimate that I would ever hire you again?" I saied, "Sorry." And that was the end of it. Hard to believe.

CHAPTER 18

MAKING A LIFE

There did seem to be a gradual build-up of delusions that began in me around the clerical guild strike in 1975. Back then I felt unusually elated, like I was invincible. Along with my alcoholism, maybe that was one symptom of the impending mental illness. I was having a lot of fun, meeting all sorts of new people. Then drunkenness added to a genetic predisposition for schizophrenia must just have been too much tempting of fate. And most psychiatrists agree that there has to be at least a "seed" there biologically to produce a schizophrenic person.

The months of discussions between Dr. Crow, Todd and me were pretty intense. The doctor had become used to our personalities. But being an M.D. instead of a psychologist didn't mean he was that much more insightful. In fact, he talked to us once a week for fifty minutes each time, and yet he did not recognize my deep depression back in spring 1982.

He may have thought I was a whining type. But that wasn't a general aspect of my personality before the mental breakdown. But now depression was presenting itself to me in a not so subtle way. I counted down the weekdays with a glimmer of hope that the weekend would bring some happiness or relief. And then on the weekends I would mourn the passage of time. I summed up my feelings about that to Todd and said, "My life has become just weeks and weekends."

That April 1982, I had gotten a job working for a women's rights group which was located next door to where Todd's job was. Deciding to look in that area to find another job, it turned out that my friend Pang Lee started there the same day as me. One of those coincidences that seem almost eerie. I became a receptionist with ten incoming lines. My boss called it "the hot seat." Pang Lee started the same day working as a typist.

162

I tried to feel my way through that job, striving to be efficient. But people didn't like to be asked anything except their name. Some of them were well-known and didn't like my saying, "And who are you with?"

It was very hectic and I barely had time to smoke the many cigarettes I lit up. After being there a week, my depression led me to ask our supervisor whether Pang Lee and I could switch jobs, since Pang Lee's job was low-keyed compared to mine. Although we had both agreed to the change, our boss said Pang Lee could never be a receptionist with her strong Korean accent. My boss asked me if I was going to stay, and I said I would.

For lunch I would either go with Pang Lee to the cafeteria around the corner from our office, or I'd go with Todd to a bar/restaurant near the paper factory. One time when Pang Lee and I were looking for jobs we went back inside the paper factory. I would obviously never work there again. I wouldn't want to and they wouldn't want me either.

Being employed could have worked out a lot better if I had not been so down. I even brought up suicide with Dr. Crow one Saturday, and he said he wasn't surprised. But he must have felt I could talk my way out of the things that made me sad, but that just wasn't happening. I'd like to know why he never suggested that I should go on antidepressants. He listened to me while I complained and discussed how terrible everything was in my life, and he never brought up clinical depression.

It was another one of those situations where I could have ended up dead. The first time was the lack of insight on the part of the Ph.D. student and his dissertation advisor at Tydings who had listened to weekly audio tapes of me and my story. I might have just continued starving myself while in that apartment for two or three more days that next summer, bringing about the end. In the Dr. Crow case, I might have bought the gun I had thought about so often. Then again, I probably could never have bought one anyway after already being committed to a mental institution. Happily, I had luck on my side with Pang Lee, who was a devout Christian. I kept discussing, as a rhetorical question, whether suicide was a mortal sin. Could you still go to Heaven? Pang Lee insisted, over a three-week period, that I could not go to Heaven if I committed a murder, even if it was myself. Since I took this line of questioning very seriously, Pang Lee ultimately saved my life. And I must admit that I wasn't giving her much back, just deeply depressed reactions to what was going on in our lives.

More relief would soon be on the way, after I had seen a "20/20" television show the night before one of the Dr. Crow discussions. The program showed people who were clinically depressed. I identified with them; the forlorn words, the deadpan faces, the postures, the lack of motivation.

Then "20/20" followed these same people far enough into their futures to be able to see what anti-depressant medication could do. The images were strong: a slight smile, a new voice, gleaming, rested faces on the same people who I had identified with at the beginning of the TV segment. I was sure that's what I needed, and when I went with Todd into that weekly session with Dr. Crow the next morning, I was armed with that new-found revelation. I told him that I was on the wrong kind of medication and wanted to switch.

Dr. Crow had a revelation of his own. A whole array of different neuron-transmitters are involved with depression than with schizophrenia. Consequently, I could be on an anti-psychotic and an anti-depressant at the same time. I question why didn't he tell me this before, as devoid of hope or happiness I was during my despondency in May 1982. But talking to Dr. Crow, with Todd there too, it was amazing that we were all going to turn a corner in about three weeks once I had been on an anti-depressant named Imipramine for that long.

Dr. Crow had said the medication would take about six weeks, since I had to build up to the correct dose during the first three weeks. So, I only knew I was getting better in a way that I couldn't yet feel. But by the time I was on the full 200 mg, I finally became a little happier. Having it only take three weeks was a surprising, added bonus.

Once I felt that relief, I was encouraged by Todd to quit my job with the women's group and start at Tydings in the continuing education college to get a computer science degree. Todd thought he had found something for me to excel at. Even his mother said, "Well, you can't go wrong with computers." That was a very welcome bit of optimism. And I went for it, signing up for as many classes as I felt I could handle.

Partly because my sister Karen had a son who was dying of leukemia, I wanted to go back for a visit and hoped my family would look forward to seeing me. My father said the nephew was very close to dying, and to hurry if I wanted to see him. I said I would.

I was ready to make a plane reservation when my sister Ellen called to try to talk me out of going to Phoenix at that time. She must have remembered the phone call Todd had me make to Marie and Eddie in Spring, 1982, asking if they were willing to let me come live with them, which was embarrassing to all of us. Ellen probably also remembered I had practically done the same thing when I lived in Milwaukee in 1972. So it was understandable that she called. I had just quit a job and maybe would foist my troubled life on my parents. That was nothing any of the people involved would like to have happen, including me. In any case, I called Matthew's father and asked him if he would mind if I visited Phoenix. He said he didn't.

Another thing that happened was that I was having a lot of difficulty with my computer science courses. For one thing, I was taking beginning and intermediate courses at the same time, for the sake of expediency, and wasn't going to make it. I was severely depressed during that monumental effort at Tydings, which caused a big disappointment. So I dropped out and lined up a new job with some engineers before my trip. That was also something my sister Ellen must have liked. "So, you have a job lined up?" she remarked. The affirmative answer helped my case; I would be given the OK to visit. Such was my standing with my family.

When my mother and sisters, Marie and Jane, met me at the airport, the first thing they said after hugs, was that Matthew had died earlier that morning. He had been told by his doctor the day before, that there was nothing he could do to help, that he was going to die. This, along with my despondency, made for a bad visit. I whined about Eddie and Marie not having me over every night. And I got drunk and spilled a beer in my mother's living room. My saddest feeling was that I had no children of my own, although Todd and I were trying to change that. I even talked to him long-distance about it.

Once I got back to Washington, D.C., I started working at the engineering firm that dealt with designing sewer systems. I read novels in between busy times when I had to type tables. This was before personal computers. I also went to the grocery store during the workday to buy coffee, filters, hot chocolate, etc. With my still being a smoker, one of the engineers insisted that they buy an air filter machine to draw out the smell that he hated. But most everyone was very nice to me during those days.

It was about this time that I had that dark cloud of depression lifted from my life. My first sense of it was when Todd and I went to the Dunkin' Donuts near Crow's office. I thought, "Yum, a blueberry muffin!" Going there had become part of a routine I followed, and that day it felt good. I told Todd about it and that made him happy too.

During my free time at my new job, I also got to type personal correspondence if I wanted to. As a result, my sister Casey, who lived in Georgia, and I became pen pals in a way. We wrote letters back and forth about our lives, our latest books and our opinions about the world. I read a lot of John Irving and also some books by southern authors that Casey recommended. It was fun.

One time Casey wrote about a night when she and a few of her sorority sisters met some fraternity men at a bar and went home with them to listen to music. I wrote that I would not have come out of that sort of evening unscathed. Casey was safe, though, inside the Greek setting, though she didn't come out and say so. It was a world I would never know. We just had two different frames of reference.

Since watching the "20/20" television show, Todd and I had continued trying to have a baby. But during my 38-day fast, my menstrual periods had stopped. I had a pregnancy test done in February 1982, but it was negative and that made me feel disappointed.

My obstetrician/gynecologist knew what kind of medication I was taking and why, and he said to go for it. First, though, he made me go through about four different tests to be sure the problem was just my not ovulating. He thought that's what the problem was. We knew the infertility problem was with me.

The last test to determine the problem was a brain scan, with an IV of iodine to pinpoint whether there was a problem with my pituitary gland. Todd and I were visiting his sister in Illinois the morning the results were to be in. I called my doctor, and he asked where I was calling from. He said "So far, so good, the way is clear for us to start you on Clomid." (Which causes ovulation.) I was so excited, as was Todd. One more hurdle over with.

While all of this was going on, Dr. Crow seemed obsessed and said things like "You know the baby will have a 12 percent chance of being schizo-affective."

Basically, Todd and I just said, "So what? He or she has an 88 percent chance that it won't happen."

Crow persisted. He had the nerve, just before I started to get on Clomid, to call my OB/Gyn himself, and tell him that I had had two psychotic breaks in the past, noting the medication I was on. Dr. Crow added that he wasn't sure that Todd really knew what he was getting into, in spite of all his statistics.

I broke down when I heard this from my obstetrician. I sobbed over the phone to Crow that he had nerve to take a step like that. In fact, the only thing that wasn't surprising, was that we continued seeing him after that. Dr. Crow told me that he would have to hear it explicitly from Todd that upcoming Saturday that he was sure he wanted to have a baby with me. Todd said "Yes, why else all the tests? Absolutely."

So Crow called my OB doctor back and said he changed his mind and to go ahead and start with the Clomid. My OB doctor was angry with Dr. Crow, especially after he had me return for a second blood chemistry test, saying that the results are often inconclusive. I told him it was a blood test, not a urine test, but Crow still hadn't meddled enough. He had me go back. Also, I remember when we called my parents to give them the good news, my father said, "Didn't your doctor tell you you shouldn't have a baby?" That hurt me a lot.

When the final word from the tests came in, I started taking hormones to start menstruation, then one tablet of Clomid about seven days later. That didn't work and I was very upset. But we tried it again, this time with two tablets of Clomid. It worked—I was pregnant. It was thus far the happiest day in my life when I got to call Todd from the engineering firm to tell him "You're going to be a father by next July." There were no words to explain the joy of it.

When I next went to see my obstetrician, he asked me, "So what's new?" We both laughed. He was happy for both of us and even had us come in to see the baby's dot of a heartbeat on a ultrasound after just one month. He said the reason for the test was to find out if it would be a single birth or multiple, given that we had used a fertility drug. It also seemed that he was just being sweet. Todd and I were thrilled. Added to the news about the baby, I was no longer under a dark cloud, thanks to the Imipramine.

But, Dr. Crow still hadn't run his course with me. Once we got the second blood test results, he decided I should no longer be on either of my medications, anti-psychotics or anti-depressants. He said they could be harmful to the baby, at least

168

in the first trimester, though there had been no conclusive tests about that. My OB/Gyn disagreed with that move, but Todd said, "Why not try it? Anne might not be mentally ill anymore."

After a few weeks, the depression and psychosis were starting to come back. With no Prolixin and no Imipramine, that should have been predictable, but I didn't know at first what to think. I was doing some very strange things—like going home to talk to Todd during my workday; I just "knew" he was really there and thought he was just not answering the phone. Rushing back and forth.

I could have simply called Todd at work, but didn't want to give away that I knew about all of "those things," whatever they were. After I had done that two times, and felt confused and odd, I summoned Dr. Crow on his beeper to call me "immediately." I wanted my medication back. I said, "Please help, I'm not doing well, I'm getting suspicious."

Dr. Crow ended up calling me brave, but that wouldn't have helped much if I hadn't stopped myself before going over. Again, why was the man still my psychiatrist? Todd and I wondered about that later. I had caught myself just in the nick of time. Thankfully, my brain chemistry was evened out again shortly after.

My sister, Marie, said to me years later, "You never sought help and wouldn't have," but there was one example. I felt myself get paranoid again, and put a stop to it. And there were other times I "rescued myself" later. Once in 1990, in Slide Rock in Sedona, I had an especially embarrassing yelling episode where the crowd stopped cold listening to me yell at Philip over and over to stop diving off the cliffs. It scared me to death. But I knew then that I needed a higher dose of Prolixin for my mental health because I was devastated by the scrutiny of the crowd. Maybe anyone would have been, but I became extremely paranoid.

One issue that came up was my drinking. I had continued to overdo it all the way up to the pregnancy. There was even one week where I snuck a few beers at lunch while working for the engineering firm, knowing I wasn't going to drink much at home anymore. That was the week both Todd and I knew there was a chance that I could already be pregnant.

People would tell me later that if I had kept up my drinking, I would have been taking a big chance, but I remember asking my OB/Gyn whether alcohol was allowed and he said, "Two or three drinks a day are OK." So people said that to me in hindsight. Except for parties I had been pretty good about that whole issue/behavior. I really clung to my three-a-day portion though. It wasn't until January 1987 that I finally gave up that habit altogether. Becoming pregnant happened in September 1982.

Suddenly there was some new good news from Todd. He found a federal job in Phoenix, Arizona—my hometown. I couldn't believe my luck and almost gloated about it to Dr. Crow, who could barely hide his feelings, saying, "Well, you certainly got what you wanted, being pregnant and moving to Arizona." He probably hated to lose his grip on us. I'm glad we got away. Todd and I went out for seafood, and I remember ordering sauteed flounder. We were both elated, and I had one of my glasses of wine for the day.

There was truly an effort on my part to keep the drinking moderate when I was pregnant. My friends were very happy for me. James said, "Congratulations on being pregnatized." Things looked rosy, and my time at the engineering firm drew to a close.

My boss also said he was glad I would get to live by my family. He said to make sure to come to the Christmas party anyway, which Todd and I did. It was quite a feast: jumbo shrimp cocktail, filet mignon, the best of everything.

Before I left D.C., I went for one last visit with my obstetrician. He told me to be sure to send a picture, and set me up to see a OB/Gyn in Phoenix. He congratulated me on our long road to success in making me fertile, and said he was glad I would be starting a new life.

Todd and I also went to see Dr. Crow one last time. It had definitely been an eventful ten months or so. And we had had quality discussions with him about mental illness, and had seen me rise out of depression and psychosis. He spoke to Todd first when giving his goodbyes, shook his hand and congratulated him about all of his luck. Then he took my hands and said something very sobering. "You have the strength to stand up to this disease. I know you're strong, and because of that, I know you will succeed." It was a nice gesture, but I was still glad to get away from his grip.

Todd and I had our last nights before leaving with both James and Karl. It was Karl who had told Todd about the job opening in Phoenix, and the three of us went to a Japanese restaurant to celebrate. James took us at another time to a seafood restaurant and I ate lobster. The moving van came the next morning, heading for Phoenix, Arizona one more time.

The evening after the moving van came to transport our belongings, Pang Lee and her husband came over to Todd's and my empty house. They brought a little cassette player with tiny speakers and we had some good conversation. It actually looked better in there with all of the furniture gone. You could see all of the finished oak floors. I wasn't very sorry the next morning to get up and be out of there, though. I had never really liked that house.

So, once again, Todd and I were on our way out of the Washington, D.C. area. We first went to Todd's hometown of Milwaukee before heading to Phoenix. Everyone there congratulated us about the baby and they didn't seem to think anything wrong with two or three glasses of wine or beer a day that I drank. I clinged to what Dr. Crow and our OB/Gyn doctor had said, that it was OK. Years later, though, it would be common to hear from doctors that no amount of alcohol was safe for pregnant women. Even back in December, 1982, there were some doubters about my easy attitude. That, along with the heavy smoking, which I didn't give up until February 1991.

Todd and I arrived in Phoenix right after Christmas. My sister, Marie, had said in a letter that "it would be great" for us to move out there. Since I wasn't getting any other opinions, I held onto that encouragement in making such a huge move. We stayed at my parents' house for about a week before we moved into a tiny apartment nearby.

Todd and I would go to visit Marie and Eddie each week to play cards, and on a few occasions I ended up drinking more than three drinks. Even getting drunk a few times. This, of course, left a lasting impression on others that I was being very irresponsible. I felt guilty later, as I should have.

It ended up being so tense a situation, that after a while Todd and I weren't invited over any more. Eddie just had the one day off most weekends because he was a mail carrier, and Saturday night was their only chance to party on the weekend. Understandably, they didn't want to be referees in a fight.

Meanwhile, both Todd and I had new jobs to go to soon after our arrival. Todd was an economist downtown and I had signed up once again with the clerical pool. Todd drove to work with Jane, one of my sisters, and I drove our Escort to the capitol area. Unfortunately, my new boss decided, either after reading my application, or the first time she saw me, that she didn't like me at all. Maybe it was because I was heavy, or because I had a college degree, but it was an unspoken animosity that charged the air. To make matters worse, the boss forged a new friendship with the other clerical pool employee who began there the same day.

For secretaries' day, the boss took us both out to eat and I drank a Margarita. That was the negative thing the boss focused on about me that day. It was funny, years later, when I had a fairly prestigious job, I ran into that woman again in a cafeteria. She was unpleasantly surprised that I hadn't used her as a "reference," but I had known better. From the spring of 1983, all I would later list about that time was "the clerical pool" and as my supervisor, the name of the head of the pool. That worked just fine. I had escaped.

My baby was due around July 5, 1983, and I didn't want to be in a micro-apartment for that occasion. So Todd and I found a house to rent near my mother and sister Marie. I had gone regularly for doctor visits with my OB/Gyn and felt sure that the baby would be perfect, no doubt unlike what some other people thought.

I had kept working for that woman with the attitude problem, so when I was "no longer needed" for the job in May 1983 I wasn't unhappy at all about leaving. Tongue in cheek, my boss said "Come by and show us your baby when it's born."

In any case, I stayed in the clerical pool but just shifted to another agency with a much friendlier group of people. When the woman who had gone on vacation returned, my fellow workers gave me some presents for the baby.

All during this time, I maintained my three drink per day schedule. My new doctor agreed. Further, when he, also a Ph.D., said that there were no tests on my kind of medication to show that the anti-depressants or anti-psychotic drugs cause birth defects, I took this encouragement to heart. And being pregnant wasn't painful to me at all, and I had no bad side effects from the combinations of chemicals I took in.

I had heard that milk is good for mothers-to-be, so I would get up in the middle of the night to drink two big glasses of chocolate milk. Later I heard that even that was not recommended, because of the caffeine in chocolate. Still, I felt fine but I was also getting impatient.

One other person who played a role in how 1983 unfolded was my old psychiatrist who worked at Belair in October 1981 when I was a patient there. Dr. Crow had recommended that we go to somebody else since my Belair doctor had diagnosed me as a paranoid schizophrenic. Crow thought that very wrong, that "He was just taking into account intelligence."

I didn't know what that meant, and furthermore I was still angry with Crow. So we went in to see the Belair psychiatrist who was a nice burley man and had a lot of background material about me. He wondered what in the world Dr. Crow discussed with us for 50 minutes every Saturday.

The three of us decided that we would start out having appointments every six weeks, which ended up being every six months. But he had served me well while I was on that type of health insurance, and I liked the idea of moving further from what Dr. Crow had in mind when he wrote the letter for me to give to a new psychiatrist.

With all of this in mind, Todd and I were pretty happy people. We wanted so much to see the baby in those ultrasound pictures though.

On the day before June 22, I had worked at a new clerical pool job where I transcribed on a dictaphone the minutes of certain meetings. No matter how hard I strained to hear, I couldn't make out some key words, Still, I tried to do my best. Needless to say, that was not an ideal job.

That night, at about 2:00 am, my side of the bed got flooded. I jumped up and cried, "Todd, my water broke!"

Of course, there was no way I was going to go back to sleep, so I talked to Todd and looked at one of my astrology books. Our baby would be a "Cancer with the moon in Sagittarius." Who knows what all that means either, but at the time I cared. I didn't get to drink my chocolate milk because the doctor said only clear liquids, so I sat there drinking diet cola, knowing that I would have the baby that day. They had told us to come in later that morning.

It definitely looked like a C-section delivery, so all the nurses would let me have all day were some ice chips. But after an epidural, I quickly became ready for the baby to arrive, around 10 p.m.

In route to the delivery room, my doctor said I was brave to have gone through all of that long labor. Todd had his camera ready for pictures of the baby afterwards, but he was too nervous to get it right. They handed the baby to me and I just said "Philip." Todd got to hold him too.

Seconds later, they whisked the baby away for his own check-up. I said, "Is the head too small?" I had heard that it means there is some retardation.

The doctors said, "His head is just the right size and he is a nine on the Apgar Scale." I didn't find out until later that for that score they checked: heart rate, respiratory rate, muscle tone, color and reflexes. They told me that meant our baby was very healthy.

They gave me back the baby. Todd and I would always remember, as well as my parents who came to see him that night, that Philip had a little conehead which would disappear by the next morning. But it was so prominent on the night he was born, we worried a little. We didn't think to take any pictures of it, though. We called everyone with the information to cheer about: he was born at 10:13 p.m. on June 22, 1983, he weighed five pounds nine ounces, and was 19 inches long. Perfectly healthy.

The next morning, I was up and about as if nothing physical had happened. There I was with the baby wrapped up in a receiving blanket on my bed beside me. I just kept staring at him, and was alone with him for about two hours. My family came by later with a bottle of champagne, and I was glad I could drink and not have to feel guilty. Todd was there with me while my family members each held Philip, commenting about how tiny he was.

So it had worked out that we could have a perfect baby, in spite of me in a way. Of course, there's always a question mark there about whether or not he will inherit my mental illness. He has a 88 percent chance that he won't. And it isn't such a bad experience that I wish I had never been born. In a later psychotic break, my mother said that Philip had been "born behind the eight ball." Nothing could have hurt me more. And nothing could have been less true.

Todd took a picture of me holding Philip in front of the hospital, and I looked very proud. But having the baby had really been the easy part, as I've discovered. Staying well for him has been the more remarkable accomplishment. And luck has usually been on my side. And I hope it always will be on Philip's side as he grows older.

CHAPTER 19

AFTER EFFECTS

Surely the whole process of me slowly becoming consumed with worrying at college developed for a reason. I really wanted there to be a <u>reason</u>. And it might just go back to the question of "Was I always 'different'?" And what does that warn me about my son Philip? He certainly seems "normal" to me. He is an interesting person, though, I'll give you that. And he's often wrapped up in his own little world inside our computer room; playing Starcraft and chatting on line with his friends at the same time.

He's always been very good at almost anything he tries to do, maybe with the exception of gymnastics. But he was great at playing the clarinet in the band, which he did for five years before admitting that he didn't even like his instrument. He has also played the piano for about seven or eight years altogether. He's "talented," his teachers sometimes say. He even took "cross country" in his freshman year at high school. He was very determined and focused during his runs, from what I could see.

In any case, he's a pretty typical 18 year old, staying up all night and of course being totally into something that's almost eccentric in its own right—"anime." (Japanese animation and the music that goes with it.) I think it's great that he's been able to narrow his focus down to what he considers entertaining. He has a stereo system with big speakers in the computer room for him to play anime music among other types of songs. And he's "cool," likes all types of <u>good</u> music. He says don't go planning his life for him though, even if he does have a definite fascination with Japan. In fact he even went there this summer! What an overwhelming process the exchange student program turned out to be.

But in the end Philip has only about a 12 percent chance of becoming a schizophrenic, though I tell him not to take his mental health for granted. Just reading this book is probably the best thing I could "say" to him about the whole experience. Once lately he asked, "Did you just <u>lose</u> yourself when you were crazy?" I guess that's a good question, or at least a good way of putting it.

Also, I must admit that he has maybe had to experience certain bizarre things that other children haven't. Like once when he and Todd made a run for it to get away from me during a psychotic break after I stopped holding onto him after about 15 minutes. I had been aftaid to let him go, though I certainly was not harming or insulting him in any way. But they jumped over a wall to get away. Of course he was just a five year old at the time, but I wonder how much of that sort of thing he remembers.

Also, I was a drunk, and he had to live with that until he was three and a half years old. What he tells me now is that he thought that I just wouldn't wake up. He remembers how he felt frustrated by that. Now he knows I was passed out, not sleeping, and I could do some worrying about him knowing all of these things if I wanted to. Sometimes I'm concerned with my motherhood "legacy," which sounds ridiculous, but that's one small reason I try so hard. One thing about schizophrenia is that it does sometimes seem like an ultimate ego trip.

Of course being a drunk had become a huge problem for me; that and overt stress was just too much for me to handle. And my family thinks my "situation" was not so much a question of an inherited chemical imbalance in my brain as it was an offshoot of my "personality" as it developed over the years.

One strange experience for Philip was me asking him during one psychotic break what was the "story" with Malcom. Now whether or not he remembers this I have no idea. He answered about someone like an imaginary friend. "He lives with his mom." And of course I took that very seriously. And that "pretend" answer from him played into my system of paranoia during the summer of 1987, six months after I gave up alcohol. That very next psychotic break sort of developed during that time, when I felt that I was really getting to the heart of the saga with Professor Collins.

Yes, my delusions said that maybe the woman who got mad at Marie for calling him that one time in October 1981 to ask his wife (presumably) what was what from Anne Bergeron might really have been Malcom's mother. And then I thought, now did she have an "old" voice, etc. (Things can really get twisted with paranoid schizophrenia.)

Also, during one break, when some of my family was out in front of our house, I told Philip not to worry because his "real dad" was out front. (Collins and I never even shook hands.) My brother-in-law, who was in the house trying to get Philip away from me, gasped when he heard that. I said, "Well, he looks just like Malcom Collins." Ernie said "He looks like Todd."

That's one I've tried to live down over the years with my family. My father had actually asked me that one summer "What part could he have played?" when I told him that Philip was younger than the number of years since I had seen Collins. I've been such an idiot at times. Either that or Philip was an "immaculate conception." And I don't think so.

I also remember being at St. John's mental hospital during my last hospital stay in summer 1989, 12 years ago, and having the six-year-old Philip come in to see me with his new sandals, bought by my mom. Also, he had his hair combed a "new way." I wonder about how much he knew about what was going on. Every time during these tragedies I asked myself nervously, "Will they 'let me' take him back?" I was so scared people were going to try to take Philip away from me. I already have enough problems to mull over.

Yes, this will be a book I can always pick up and open any page and the words would be exactly what I had in my mind about the times when I was psychotic. And I will have written them down. I guess the puzzle would be how my mind would interpret this book if I had another psychotic break. Let's hope I never have to find out.

So I'll never have a resolution of this problem about who feels what or who is sympathetic about me being in an awkward position as a schizophrenic. I remember after one break I asked my sister Marie if she thought I was a "bad mother." She said probably the worst thing she could have: "I don't know. I'd have to read more about it." Very untactful. But what do I expect? Mentally ill people in general certainly don't get much respect.

All in all, I think the after effects for Philip are that he knows that I've become psychotic several times and unfortunately can never be considered really "cured." That's my fate. I think Philip also realizes that with both parents having clinical depression, he might need medication like that some day too. In fact, he one time suggested Prozac. I'm not sure where he read about it, but he did say at the time that he felt "more energy" because of it. That's in the past, and he does best now without any type of drug. I guess we almost started him on the drug therapy roundabout at a very young age.

There might be a realization with him about schizophrenia, but I don't really know. Like I've said, he remembers very little about my past mental problems. I think he is more worried about becoming an alcoholic. He says he'll never drink, smoke or take any drugs. He was going to take "Health" as one of his electives as a junior in high school, but it was cancelled for lack of interest. I guess he'll be a very straight arrow. Not the type to wear an earring.

But in the end Philip is basically aloof about most personal things. Or at least he pretends to be. And he really loves his privacy. I actually like Philip's somewhat detached personality. He's a "free spirit" in certain ways, and that makes me think that he will always let things roll off his back. Kind of a "If they don't like me, to hell with them" attitude. I could certainly use that type of sentiment. He is the opposite of me, never really worries to any great extent about anything. And he has been improving his self-confidence as time marches on at high school, where he memorized his presentations to the class so well last year that he got 100 percents for doing so. And last year he took speech, getting an A. That's something I'm proud of him for doing. I think many people, including me, ought to have taken speech in high school.

Often though, he keeps tied up within his world of school, computers and anime. He's taken two years of Japanese at school, and is devoted to the movies made about the big-eyed, soft and interesting anime characters in these films. It's a great thing for him to be "into."

He also used to listen to anime music on his headphones in the car in addition to while he'd be on the computer. And he's a leader in his small group of friends; that makes me happy. And one year he made more friends all the time in part because of a new "anime club." He was the real "guru" in that group, though he doesn't want to come out and say so. But I know it's something he's proud of.

All in all, I think Philip will have a very successful life. Anything he could gain from having been doted on his entire life will be there for him. He sometimes wonders out loud how he would have turned out if I hadn't done any drinking or smoking when I was pregnant. It's hard to imagine that he could have turned out better. Thank God for that one!

***

Todd has basically found himself in talks with me and my psychiatrists many times over the years. The Dr. Crow thing was definitely a dual effort. And he's gone in with me so much that some of these conversations seem almost natural to him. And then of course keeping an eye on me and my depression led him to become more aware of his own depression when it began in 1984.

Back then he felt despairingly out of touch with Matthews University at a time where it was mandatory that he take a daytime class there three times a week in "macro" economics. Then that's when I went to the class required for his master's degree and took notes while recording the class on a small tape recorder. I did this while Todd took care of Philip for those hours every week. Looking back I'm glad I got to add that effort to our long-term relationship. But I don't think I could do it again.

On the other hand, I think he has a lot to learn about chronic mental illness. He's always felt that the sessions were about me, not him, even when they were. But we've both learned about prejudice towards mental illness like more people are becoming aware of all the time with insurance companies. We both think all of the "clauses" about mental illness are unethical—especially with HMO's.

One big predicament for the two of us is that Todd has always been concerned with me having a "paying job," while it's just something I always screw up since graduating from college. I know he grew up in a family where making money was considered a "responsibility" for him and his siblings. At an early age, Todd was out there making money by mowing lawns for his neighbors. Then he may even have had a newspaper route. He has one sister who is following the pattern perfectly with her own sons. Todd's parents are tuned into that real heavily. Philip should not have a car unless he pays for it, if you want something, work for it, etc. I think it's good for them to be so sure that they're right. They were certainly right about me being an alcoholic during that North Carolina Christmas visit to Raleigh fiasco in 1980. Though it took me a long time to get over their presentation of their opinions. I'm sure nobody has totally forgotten that awful scene. But Todd has a lot to offer. He loves me very much, I think I can say that. And he's always loved this book, even when I was ashamed of it. I've helped him in life and he's helped me. We always say in our cards that we've been through so much together, both good and bad. That without a doubt is true. And we both have parents who have been together over 50 years! Maybe that's a good omen. We disagree a lot about how to spend money, and I have heard that's the topic most important to the success of a marriage. But we must be doing something right; we've been together for about 28 years.

But all three of us are good about money. I do realize we're a "one wage-earner family" as Todd often points out. We visit bookstores often, and instead of buying the many books we're interested in we take down the title and author and check them out of the library. And nobody can compete with Todd on "thriftyness" if you let him have his way. Which also means he's very good at managing our money.

As I've said, there was the conundrum of my working at jobs I couldn't stand. I heard one of my 1990 bosses say about me behind my back, "Can you believe those shoes she wore on her interview? She'll be here until she rots." I was so unhappy, so bad at whatever I tried to do, except maybe for typing letters. But Todd and his parents always made sure I knew their opinions about that subject. And so in those days I stayed, miserably.

Todd is also enthusiastic about the internet, wants everyone to communicate on-line. Even though his parents asked him to quit trying to talk them into buying a computer, he and his sister bought them an e-mail machine last year and they <u>love</u> it. So there's something to be said for persistence.

His class project at Matthews University last semester was "Internet Green," a cornocopia of some of his ideas with pictures and some interesting stories about people using the internet. No doubt Todd has quietly done a lot of soul searching through his art, and he's a good "artsy" type of person. His major, "interdisciplinary arts" is a lot to even enunciate.

When I first met him in 1973, right before I was working at the post office, he was so sure that within ten years mailmen would be out of business. He wasn't right on that one. Though of course, think about e-mail and how that has changed communication for everyone logged onto a computer. Even I think it's a fun experience to be into that sort of thing.

But what to do about the "money" thing? We're in a bit of a let's be unhappy "situation," like I said, though Todd has become less concerned about the job thing ever since Christmas 1999. But I'm often out of the mainstream of decision making. However, the way I feel these days? Mellowed out about the whole damned thing. There's too much good going on to be sad.

One thing is that I'm afraid of confrontation. I can't walk away. I've learned from watching TV and movies that one person says something to another person and then walks away. It gets resolved later. But I'm too afraid to leave things to chance—I think it stems from having Todd walk away and hiding Philip from me when I was last in a mental hospital. That was after me lying to get into the hospital so Todd and I wouldn't get a divorce. Lied just like he had wanted, because I loved my little family. He had promised we wouldn't break up if I went voluntarily to St. John's for that last psychotic break 11 years ago. And probably a lot of people would think he did the right thing in that regard, even the part about leaving me. Not my family, but his.

***

I got really embarrassed about my book when I was working with an agent who never even wanted to meet me face to face. She wouldn't let me write "He got kicked in the butt." She said you have to say "buttocks." Just one little bad habit of hers was to want to be in charge. How do I draw these types of people to me? Maybe I'm a control freak too. I know Philip and Todd are.

But I'll call the agent "Betty." Well, she liked to mark up my manuscript, but she just wasn't very informed. Also she said that she was "Sick to death of my story." Imagine what that did to my ego. She wanted me to write a book about pioneer women or a "textbook" on Native American women. What a laugh. And I paid her $900, after which she discontinued working to get the book published.

She said after somebody picks up a different effort of mine they might consider publishing "In Whose Eyes?" as a courtesy to me as the writer of a "published" book. It's because of her that I abandoned the manuscript for about five years. What a waste of having a good time writing. This book is my always enjoyable foray into the art of literature which could go on indefinitely if I was a perfectionist.

One fairweather friend is my sister Marie. She was the only person I let read my book except for Todd and his mother. She heard me say that one publisher said it wasn't "strong," the only hint ever given me by Betty about what any client might have said. So I let a few months pass, and when I said "Did you think it was a good book?" She replied, "Except for the first three chapters it just wasn't 'strong' enough." Who knows though? Maybe it's true.

I've said if I were to write another book it would be about this same subject. Both Betty and Marie said, "This book and subject is a 'hard sell' Please move on. This has been a catharsis for you." I say never say die. I'll keep on striving.

And maybe this kind of attitude from the two of them was partly necessary to get a decent effort out of me, even though it's years later. But neither Marie or Betty ever encouraged me about the book at all once the effort was definitely on its way to some conclusion. I spent all kinds of time being embarrassed by my own writing. And now everyone forgets about those five years on the shelf and thinks I've been obsessing about this manuscript since 1992. Then again, who cares about the flinging of disparagements my way? I do of course, but I hate to admit it. So I go through life now feeling like a "younger" woman, but only in one way. I admit that I've had some erosion of my intellect. And my memory has gotten pretty bad. But I'm always anxious for the good things to happen. I know very little as far as mathmatics or economics goes—my main emphasis in college.

That megadose of departmental "dishonor" will never truly be out of my life. That was there for me at one time, and I carry that experience with me always for what it's worth. Todd sometimes says I wasted his money going to college, that type of thing. But I've grown to like my past.

One of my only real weapons is this book, though I've redone the manuscript so many times. My only innate talent is writing about the facts of my life and those people I've interacted with. I've asked people whether or not writing a memoir is the most egotistical thing you can do. Some say yes, but most do not.

I can be pushy when I have to be, but I'm so uneloquent on my feet it's a shame. Everyone has a lot to say if they'll just say it, I guess. But I'm even very bad at picking funny gifts for turning 40 or 50 parties. As one example of my loss for words, it even took me years to realize a few obvious aspects of the subject of my own book.

In any case, my son will move to a dormitory next fall 2002. It will be a big adjustment. I guess I'll have to start "doting" on Todd. He probably deserves it for all he's been through. I figure it must have been hard on Todd's ego all of my "fantasizing" about other men. He deserves more certainty than that. And I'll have my son and my book to be proud of creating along with our quite long marriage, which has to be considered at least a passable "success." We'll look into each other's eyes to find pictures that we've both seen. And more gentle moments. That might make me happy enough to get by.

And I'll sometimes be in my room with all of my books, especially those library books I've renewed about 20 times. And I'm also waiting for that phone call or letter, always cognizant of what might pass me by. It almost goes without saying.

I'll be watching for the sucess of this book, and my next will be a labor of love called "Through His Eyes" about my son Philip. He's been through a lot too. We all have. Like that one book title states "Live, Learn and Pass It On." That's a good philosophy to have. Todd and Philip deserve a great life too.

And more and more, as I've learned recently for myself, being a good mom means letting go. My son will hopefully carry with him the strength to deal with any kind of crisis that comes his way. He knows he's loved, and that's my "motherhood legacy." I'll work hard on the rest of the getting along that I need to do. It will be just Todd and me living here nine months a year in not that long. But let's hope the three of us always look forward to talking to one another. That's half the fun of life.

CHAPTER 20

HOW TO SEE IT

The definition of "schizophrenia" as described in the Webster's New World Dictionary, Third College Edition (1988) is: "A major mental disorder of unknown cause typically characterized by a separation between the thought processes and the emotions, a distortion of reality accompanied by delusions and hallucinations, a fragmentation of the personality, motor disturbances, bizarre behavior, etc., often with no loss of basic intellectual functions."

Actually this strikes me as an honest attempt by "Webster's" to provide a broad feeling for the basic definition, though some of it contradicts what I've tried to explain in this book. But every person with this illness probably shows a unique set of symptoms. For one thing, I'm a little bit annoyed that it uses words like "separation between thoughts and emotions." Someone else might agree with that. But what does it really mean?

Especially unfortunate is the phrase "fragmentation of the personality," which sounds too close to the overall worst definiiton of schizophrenia ever: "split personality." That is used universally and erroneously. The illness that refers to is "multiple personality disorder." Then again, probably every dictionary has its own take on this definition.

I also see myself in those words, however. Especially the "distortion of reality." I was filled to the brim with delusions, as I've said. And to be explicit, I do think there's <u>no chance</u> that I've outgrown it or am no longer a schizophrenic. I've accepted that as my fate.

"No loss of basic intellectual function," is partly true in my case. I can still often remember "people things," like how I felt when I lost a friend. But I also have forgotten many facts, even getting a little confused sometime with multiplication tables. On the other hand, though I am very quiet, I often have a real "feel for" my history. For example I remember exactly what was said during important parts of the cataclysmic year of experiencing the personality of Malcom Collins.

Make the definition "paranoid schizophrenia" and you just about have my situation. For over 20 years these two words have been very applicable to me. Even when I'm not in a psychotic break I can be very paranoid. It helps me to admit it.

My current psychiatrist said that having an anti-psychotic drug cease to work as mine did in 1989 was "very unusual." I certainly hope so. Things have been going well with me for over 11 years since then. So I guess I am always "significantly improved in the short run," as the HMO's like to hear.

My whole world could turn upside down if my sanity were to detonate again, so life's a little bit scary for me. Then again there are probably only a handful of people in the world who are never scared. Maybe I should take up meditation.

I haven't had a psychotic break since June of 1989—an extremely important issue to me. That happened because the Prolixin that Dr. Crow had put me on in early 1982 stopped working after seven years—at any dose. How does one prepare for that? Or what was really behind that, to be provocative. Could I have talked my way out of it?

In any case, in 1989 I was switched to Mellaril, another anti-psychotic drug, and I have been fine ever since. Of course I still consider the experience with Prolixin to be an ominous sign that this delusional free fall could happen again even after all this time. Yet, as I've said, my psychiatrist says that what happened to me and my needing to switch medications was virtually unheard of.

My hospitalizations since the initial two committments were all very brief and all with Todd's presence as my husband. Those first two breaks were my "psychosis" in the most pure form— unseen and unaware of to other people.

Anne Bergeron

Then of course I had a psychotic break in the summer of 1987, after I had my doctors try Lithium instead of Prolixin. Two more there, two in the summer of 1988 and then the one long one in 1989 when I went to St. James Hospital (private) and Todd and Philip snuck away from me in a way that I must assume was meant to be a permanent situation. Talk about feeling betrayed.

Then hallelulia the almost 12 years of uninuterrupted sanity since the summer of 1989—though one might want to check the sanity of the person insisting that I could depend upon that continuing indefinitely.

Back in the early 80's, Dr. Crow had always thought that I was "manic-depressive" rather than schizophrenic. I thought I would at least try Lithium, although I had pretty much decided that Dr. Crow was an idiot. But my decision was partly due to another psychiatrist showing me what the facial contortions of tardive dyskinesia look like if that illness strikes due to a patient taking anti-psychotic drugs. (Conspicuous and embarrassing.)

With the substitution of Lithium, I ended up back at the county hospital since I would not go "voluntarily." Back again, after seven years. People forget about that time period. The sanity had continued in-check for all that time due to Prolixin. But following that failure, one orderly even remembered me— and said so. Seven years meant nothing in certain circles.

Leading up to that, I had sat on the ground at a Grateful Dead concert with a water jug while everyone else was standing and dancing around me. I was so nervous that I had to make a decision about Philip's preschool within a few weeks. And "What about Malcom and me? Why weren't we together yet?" That implausible story seemed so significant and was so important to me. Hopefully never more important than my family.

Ultimately, the doctors put me on a higher dose of Prolixin, and I went home totally embarrassed. For those two committments, it was Karl who helped Todd carry me away to the county. It was a successful payoff to avoid my family, since I

190

was only at the clinic for one night, and Philip hadn't needed to be spirited away. And for that "involuntary" admission scene I refused to open my eyes. To be perfectly honest, I no longer know what specific delusion led to me doing that.

But Todd came into the day room to talk to me and said "They are recommending 180 days at the state hospital." That lit me up like a firecracker. Of course I would be OK! That should say something that just talking worked. I opened my eyes to see that there was nothing at all unusual going on. I was relieved, though I had let those delusions cause another commitment. Very bad news.

Karl said at one point that summer that my psychiatrists had done too much "experimenting" with me. I agreed—I did feel like a guinea pig. Two summers, two close psychotic breaks each. Dear God.

You know I think sometimes that I could have been OK all along since Tydings University if I had not been so damned quiet and shy. I find now that when I'm feeling paranoid, if I just tell the people concerned how I feel, sometimes I see their point, or that there often was nothing to be nervous about. That's a lifelong challenge for me to just speak up for myself. Of course I'm being like an alcoholic who says they can drink "moderately." Just talking to people wouldn't work in the end, and I think we all know that. But it works sometimes for me, so I'll just go with that as one recommendation.

In my case, in that following summer of 1988 once again I had those two breaks, but had my family involved. There was a birthday party for Philip, who turned five that year. One of my brother-in-laws came up and gave me a "too bad" hug. So he knew. And as I've said, it was very scary, for one thing, that people in my family seemed to have a question of whether I could get Philip back from Marie, where he had stayed most of the four committments in 1987 and 1988. I always was always worried sick about that every time I went back to retrieve him from that environment. What could they have said about me to

Philip during all those times? I don't think they've ever given me an honest answer about that.

The beginning of that second summer 1988 psychotic break had my brother, George, a Phoenix policeman, and about four of his policeman friends come into our house to see me "be crazy," I guess to entertain them; I don't know. But they all seemed in a good mood when I stated my name as "Anne Collins" and answered more of their questions. Roger asked "Who owns the title to this house?" I said Malcom Collins did. They pretended to be writing information down, as if there was some reason for them to be there. But even I can see the silliness of it, however not so much of my needing an audience.

So those four committments were brief and all about me perhaps being Malcom's wife or something equally as ridiculous. We had been "waiting so long," that kind of thing. (The story this book is about.) So I can now unfortunately state that I have been committed to the county clinic six times.

So the last time I saw that day room was in summer 1988. Of course now I know I never have the chance to see it again because it no longer stands where it was. And let there be no doubt that no matter how short the psychotic breaks were, all of them were terrifying to me if for no other reason than the taking away of Philip.

And of course I should never be in a situation where I'm <u>now</u> wondering where the "involuntary admissions" place is where I'm going to be taken. I've seen a few pictures of temporary quarters. It might as well be jail.

<u>The New Encyclopaedia Britannica</u> had an elaboration on the subject of mental illness along with a list of symptoms of schizophrenia. With me, you could always tell when one of my psychotic breaks had appeared. I had "persecutory delusions," such as believing that practically the entire economics faculty at Tydings was "out to keep me from graduating." They were "working in concert to undermine me." Paranoid, I even felt that my parents' next door neighbors had surveillance equipment in

the back yard to keep an eye on me for Malcom while I sat out back on the porch swing. These were textbook symptoms of schizophrenia.

More specifically, as described in that same source, "delusions of reference occur in schizophrenia when a patient attributes a special, irrational and usually negative (sometimes 'romantic?') significance to people, objects, or events in relation to themself." I attributed to myself much assumed knowledge about many things, but I was real "big" on Malcom Collins. I believe that he had completely set me up for a fall. But it was mostly in my imagination that he had thoughts about me to match my own thoughts about him. He probably was unlucky just by having met me, with my state of mind being as it was.

The crisis clinic psychotic breaks all seemed to happen in Phoenix in the summer, as if time of year might have some bearing. In fact, my family would point out to the doctors at the county that I must be psychotic to be sitting outside in the middle of the summer. The truth was that the heat was alright with me as long as I was in the shade.

Of course in May through July of 1989, I had my most drawn-out psychotic break since the first, before I was ever diagnosed eight years earlier. I "knew that I was OK" because no matter what dose of Prolixin they tried on me, I was still having delusions about Malcom Collins.

The songs I played on the stereo had meanings "just for me." With the Beatles' song, "The Two of Us" it had words "Two of us writing papers, getting nowhere," and I thought this was a direct message about my and Collins' charade. I also thought about the lines in "All You Need is Love" by the Beatles, with "Nothing you can know that isn't known, nothing you can see that isn't shown, nowhere you can be except where you're meant to be." I felt that this too was a personal reflection about me and Malcom; like yes, you should be feeling this way because it's true.

I didn't seem to care that these songs were written way before I ever returned to college. I also felt that Bruce Hornsby and Joe Cocker, among other rock vocalists, had my ordeal in mind with some of their songs.

Another very common symptom of schizophrenia that I displayed was written about in that New Britannica Encyclopaedia, It was that of "hearing voices speaking negatively about oneself in the third person." That was true, as when I was in the apartment in D.C., I was positive that I could make out voices of various people from ICC in the apartment across the hall talking about me. I couldn't hear the exact words, but was sure it was people from my former place of employment "watching" my actions to ascertain what was going on with me.

"Was I acting correctly?" This was what I remembered feeling. I also "remembered" Malcom Collins coming up to my door that one time just to say my name and then leave. These were all thoughts I would have during my later psychotic breaks and assume inappropriate conclusions about.

I also questioned where my belongings went that I had put down the garbage chute. It just couldn't be to the dump, I hoped. Who would allow that? I was puzzled about how things had turned out. That reference book further stated, "The schizophrenic's sense of self may be disturbed." And, that "He may withdraw from the world, becoming detached from others and become preoccupied with silly, bizarre, or nonsensical fantasies." Sounds familiar.

My "visual hallucinations" were interesting too. I swore that I saw Malcom following me in the bus behind mine that one time, when I saw him get off and follow me until I turned around, the day before the fast. I was also sure, and had told Todd, that I saw Tom Kramer, my former supervisor from ICC, visiting at a townhouse right across from ours. What was the likelihood of that?

After the psychotic break in 1989, I have to have faith that I will be all right from now on too, because I was fine after taking

"Mellaril." Luckily, it has been over 12 years since I had "no insight into my own condition and realized neither that I was still suffering from mental illness nor that my thinking was disordered." This is also from the same <u>Encyclopaedia</u>.

Of course, the psychotic breaks severely upset my sense of self-esteem, but as long as I know it could happen again, I'll be alright. The breaks are survivable, hopefully <u>with</u> Todd. Though I'm not completely sure about that.

One happy note is that I gave up drinking in January of 1987. I haven't touched a drop since, and it's actually not that hard anymore to keep away from it. I enjoy myself when others are drinking around me, but I know I could never be moderate about it again. So, I don't fear for myself in that regard. I'm just fine, and now I drink only non-alcoholic beer and wine.

Thinking back, I never had adequately considered my own actions from 1980 as perhaps being the cause of my mental struggle. I sometimes thought instead that life was just "happening to me." Now I'm sometimes fearful of the circumstances of my life becoming too stressful, which was definitely one of the causes behind what happened to me mentally. I need a lot of time to "prepare mentally" for the things I'll be doing. I'm a big list maker, plus I put everything away at night so I'll be able to find it the next day. A real control freak.

One very scary thing for me was that Todd was always preoccupied with me getting a job. I've alluded to that before. You would think an economist would think things through more thoroughly. And he knows how much higher a level I operate at when I'm not being dragged down by what for me (since being ill) is always a bad situation. In the past, my son Philip drew a picture of me with a huge cup for all the pop I drink and a huge smile on my face as well. I just pray I can keep the demons at bay; being happy for Todd and Philip is one of my goals. I honestly feel that I owe them that much.

Nothing is worse to me than my depression however. My anti-depressant medication puts a "floor" on the downside of moods that I could have, and I am acutely aware of what variables I am most vulnerable to. I shore up my mood with having a job or two that I love—being a writer as well as a wife and mother; and a lover of conversation. I'm not that good at it, but I nevertheless love "talking" to people I know well. That and beer and music used to be my thing. Now it's NA beer or soft drinks, but all else stays the same. Although I'm much better on paper, where I don't have to think on my feet, as I've mentioned as one of my weaker points.

Even when I'm not in a psychotic break, I consider myself a significant person. Maybe that's good. During one psychotic break, though, I thought everybody in the world knew everything that I had ever written down. This is much like a symptom when schizophrenics believe that people can read their minds. It was one reason why I trashed everything. Again "delusions of grandeur." Nobody is that important.

On the question of how I'm doing these days, I feel very good. I have a weight problem I need to tackle, but I'm working on that. I feel I have a sort of mission to tell people about schizophrenia, to be positive about possible outcomes for those who are stricken. And thus I wrote this book.

One thing that really undermined my spirit was when Todd left me and took Philip with him when that last psychotic break happened to me in summer 1989. That was devastating and totally uncalled for, though it had been a long episode. After a while, he let me have Philip back and then he came back too. But I would never forget the rejection that came at such an inopportune time: when I was hospitalized voluntarily "to get at the truth."

I had even faked being suicidal to my primary care physician so I would be "allowed in." Todd had asked me to do that very convincingly. The physician didn't have any options, and I was allowed in. But then the thing about Todd taking himself and Philip to a "secret hiding place" while I was in the hospital just threw me over. Luckily, I stayed away from booze as a reaction to all of those broken promises.

But at that private hospital, I "told the whole story" to a fellow patient on my first night there. I had been put on the non-working dose of 400 mg. of Mellaril a few hours before. He advised me to "Write Malcom a letter, to find out where he stands." That was after I told him that I had called Malcom just a few days earlier, and he had slammed down the receiver after saying, "Shut up!" The other patient had obviously baited me, or so I thought. Certain people are very prejudiced towards the chronic mentally ill. And one thing I showed that patient that night was that I definitely fell into that category.

But I mentioned my writing a letter to Malcom a few times to Todd the next day, when he was in a very bad mood. And Todd is very moody. Of course he wanted immediate progress, which only came the next day, after I had been on 600 rather than 400 mg. of Mellaril. But the whole turnaround point was one day too late for Todd, who had decided to cut me off totally, I think because I was still believing the "story" about me and Malcom. I cried at the hospital when I realized what had happened. I thought it showed very bad judgment, and it was an expensive "outing" for Todd and Philip, to say the least. I actually think of it as a kidnapping.

There is no cure for this disease. Negative as that is for me, I am happy that there have been certain anti-psychotic drugs to halt most of my symptoms. In fact, there are new drugs now that my doctor could "try out on me" if the Mellaril stopped working. My previous psychiatrist (who wrote the introduction) said he thought about a third of diagnosed schizophrenics lead normal lives. For me, medication had been the only real "treatment" I needed. Talking to psychiatrists and psychologists was helpful too.

It's a good idea to look for early warning signs of schizophrenia in someone you care about. I had been advised by that general practitioner at Tydings to "Go see a psychiatrist if you would like." But I didn't follow through, didn't think it was necessary. That might have been my chance for an early diagnosis. If you wait too long after delusions or depression begin, you will probably have less and less cooperation from that troubled person, leading to involuntary hospitalizations, six of which I had and will always regret having.

Keep in mind, you must never lose hope if a friend or member of the family becomes a schizophrenic, not until every drug is tried and the loved one hides from you in the streets. Even then, keep praying and try to find him or her again. Also, never let anyone you love who is committed to a mental hospital to be forgotten or ignored—no matter which institution they may be in. My life now is happy, partly because I am no longer under any kind of major duress. No more A's to get or inappropriate feelings about any man. I'm working out of my home and am contented. I get to be with Philip when he's not in school. Lucky for me. College will of course be a different situation.

My husband Todd, sometimes good-natured, has been with me as mostly a positive reinforcer of my sanity throughout most of the years since 1973 when we met. And in a way, he has benefitted greatly due to having been in on most of my psychiatric dialogue with professionals in that field. He has discovered some things about himself that have helped him with life in general, and also with being the husband of a schizophrenic. He has also come to terms with a few of his own psychological vulnerabilities.

Fortunately, our insurance carries anti-psychotic and anti-depressant medication, and they allow hospitalizations for a brief amount of time for "acute episodes." So I just take my medication with no other type of therapy. That has worked fine, so much so that I went voluntarily to that private hospital when I last became ill in summer 1989, as I've said. One thing to consider, though, is that I'm not a doctor. These have been my experiences, and anyone who displays the symptoms I talk abut should see a psychiatrist or psychologist, though sometimes they're not all infallible either.

What would happen if I were to have another psychotic break? In all other cases, I'm always "improved through relatively short-term treatment," the treatment being taking my drugs. Would I switch or increase medications or go to a hospital voluntarily? Short-term history says that I would.

I have learned by now not to "fix what isn't broken."

Experimentation has often caused a failure in my otherwise successful life. And I have no need for "Up to 30 visits a year to psychological or psychiatric counselors or doctors." This is what most other people in an HMO could demand and which is very expensive. Right now I go see a psychologist about every six weeks.

Having Philip was a beginning of a whole new life for me. I had never been so outreaching towards anybody else, certainly not any other child. Since Philip is now over 18 years old, no health problems whatsoever, one would hope that if my medication stopped working I could summon up some more of the "brave" spirit that I have shown in the past, for his sake. Especially if I started thinking Malcom Collins was anyone significant at this point in my life. That would be a morose situation.

Why didn't I know I had gone too far all those times? How could I <u>not</u> have known? This is something even my own family can't conceive. "Psychosis is a stranger," as author James Ingram Merrill once said, "What we dream up must be lived down." And it is always a long road to any sort of understanding from anyone after a mental breakdown.

But there's hope. And happiness. Somewhere beyond my rarely occurring symptoms is the me who lives a fulfilling life. I really am quite a fortunate woman, hoping to inspire others stricken with schizophrenia, depression or both—like me.

Many years have passed since my son was born, giving me a more objective point of view. Surely all my symptoms were there that lead to my initial breakdown, but nobody saw it coming. Having had psychotic episodes doesn't have to leave me helpless or despondent. It doesn't and shouldn't have to mean "the end" of anything. As you see, though, I am leery about it.

I can still go on and have a vital, creative and happy life— even if the Mellaril would stop working. Of course, that would somewhat depend on whether Todd and Philip were supportive, but I have no reason at this point to think they wouldn't be. (Then again, I'd said that before.) But as I mentioned, my current psychiatrist says that having an anti-psychotic drug cease to be effective is highly unusual. But I know it can happen, and that's my best contribution to the understanding about this illness. Of course it could also be just a quirk of my personality. Nobody knows the <u>why</u> about any of this.

I noticed psychotic breaks in the making on a few occasions where I stopped them dead in their tracks. I wrote about how I stopped one when I was pregnant. And in 1990, one year after my last hospitalization, I felt myself start to be suspicious and paranoid. Things that shouldn't bother me did, I thought everyone knew "about me," and everything was so "significant."

So I switched from 600 mg. of Mellaril a day to 700 mg. of Mellaril a day, and I had been fine since. Then in 1998 I switched to 800 mg. a day, the largest dose anyone should take. So I am a little nervous. Then again, I feel that talking myself down from a psychotic break could now be possible. Sometimes I get very paranoid, but I'm not quite as shy about admitting that anymore or asking people if what I'm thinking about them is true. So that's about as subtle as it gets. And I feel very lucky to be in that third of schizophrenics who are made well again on medication!

One thing I've noticed over the years is how few schizophrenics I see who get any respect from other patients or even from the psychiatrists and other mental health professionals. I honestly don't think we show up that much in the mainstream of society. I certainly never talked to anyone with "psychosis," the bitter pill of a word, but what else can I say? I think a lot of us are homeless or sitting in dungeons of horror somewhere. I know that seems cynical, but how often has someone admitted to being a "schizophrenic." And we're a full 1 percent of the U.S. population.

I hide it. I think most of us must hide it. It's not a good thing. But maybe this book will help. However I would no longer suggest prescribing your own dosages of medication. If I had just hung in there things that seem twisted would simply become "coincidences" or a misreading of others' emotions. So try hard to get to know one of us, you gentle reader.

Of course I need to think about the very wonderful son I've wrapped my life around. If he stays healthy, then I'll really know how lucky I am. He's read this book now, and so I'm vulnerable to him. I'm hoping that's a good thing. I just hope he handles life with as much brilliance as he's shown so far. If only life could stay this good, and maybe it can.

ABOUT THE AUTHOR

Anne Bergeron is a paranoid schizophrenic. There was no history of that in her family, which made it more difficult to first diagnose. Her schizophrenia progressed gradually over time for multiple reasons including academic pressure and alcoholism. Anne grew up in a large Catholic family. She started writing in high school and was awarded a journalism scholarship. She wasn't serious and dropped out after three semesters.

She was married at age twenty-two, her husband graduated from college, and they moved to Washington, D.C. all in the same week. She was swept away by life in the nation's capital during the 1970s—Watergate, disco, money and the good times with their many new friends. She went on strike and became an alcoholic.

When returning to college in 1978, it was kind of an "Alice in Wonderland" story where she toppled into the Mad Hatter's Tea Party. Unfortunately, she was by then always plagued by perfectionism and the stress that came with it. She lost her sanity in that endeavor.

She was involuntarily committed to mental hospitals six times over the years. She was voluntarily hospitalized the last time in 1989. She has her own family now and leads an optimistic life.

Printed in the United States
1346300001B/162